MW01592822

Published by
HARA Publishing
P.O. Box 19732
Seattle, WA 98109

Copyright @ 1998 by Josie Wannarachue
All rights reserved

ISBN 1-883697-22-0

Library of Congress Number: 98-074021

Cover design: Jennifer Wannarachue
Food Photographer: Yuttapol Vechchapinan
Design and Styling: Josie Wannarachue
Editor: Cherie Tucker

Printed in Thailand by Thai Watana Panich Press Co., Ltd.
E-mail : twpp @ bkk.loxinfo.co.th
http://www.t-w-p.com

THAI CUISINE AT ITS BEST
WITH
WINE RECOMMENDATIONS

JOSIE   WANNARACHUE

Thai Orchids

Dedication

To my quietly dignified Nikom–
  a dedicated medical doctor
  a husband whose unwavering support made all my
    endeavors possible
  a father with an inexhaustible patience for our children;

To my beautiful children who, as young Asian
Americans, have given Nikom and me much pride and
happiness-
  Jo Anne, the cosmopolitan and savvy fashion
    marketing director;
  Nathan, a first-rate athlete and a gentleman;
  Jennifer, my energetic and spontaneous artist and
    designer;
    and
  Natalie, our special angel.

And to my mother, Soledad, who is always there for me

Floating Market

Acknowledgments

I am deeply grateful to Coke Roth for sharing his many talents in wine and food. Special thanks to my official tasters: Deborah Barnard and Rob Griffin of Barnard Griffin Winery, Sharon and Ken Ferrigno, Trisha and David Gelles, Betty and Floyd Hodges, Lois McGuire, Virginia Pitts, Cathy Preston of Preston Premium Wines, and Mary and Coke Roth for their tireless efforts and discriminating tastes in choosing the perfect wines to compliment specific Thai dishes.

My special thanks go to the wineries whose products were used in the food and wine tasting: Badger Mountain Vineyards, Barnard Griffin Winery, Bookwalter Winery, Chateau Ste. Michelle, Chinook Winery, Claar Cellars, Columbia Crest Winery, Gordon Brothers Wines, Hedges Cellars, The Hogue Cellars, Horizon's Edge Winery, Kiona Vineyards Winery, Preston Premium Wines, Quarry Lake Vintners, Seth Ryan Winery, Tagaris Winery, Washington Hills Cellars, Waterbrook Winery.

Special thanks to James E. Dean for the illustrations, John Hilton of Print Plus for some of the pictures. To my niece, Massie Kalaw Santos, and Paul E. Ramin, for their technical assistance, and to Willy Zaragoza, for providing valuable insight in the revising and editing of this book.

My sincere appreciation to the following people: Becky Villacorta Aaron; Mely Alumkal; Lita Ayran; Beldad Bander; Amphan Bouttavong; Menchie Cayetano; Janet Daniels; Leony Hill; King and I Restaurant staff of Kennewick,

Washington,; Jenie Lee; Darlene Macias; Carole Mackey; Jason Mixey; Karen Osborne; Trudy Prince; Michael Richardson; Elsie and Lito Santos; Ira and Iza Santos; Kannika Soukkhammala; Luz Tuazon; Mayble Vallejo; Merle Villacorta; Cora Villanueva; and Napaporn Wannarachue.

To Zosie Padilla, Melita Cabanilla, Lettie Anel and Ophie Ante for generously sharing their time, talent and critiques, and for believing in me and in this project right from the start, and to Hara Publishing for invaluable guidance and direction.

Last but not least, to my Nikom.

CONTENTS

Map of Thailand

Introduction

Once known as Siam, Thailand is situated in the heart of Southeast Asia. Rich endowments of both natural and human resources in proportion to its population have created a standard of living that is one of the highest in Asia. Its Buddhist religion, anchored on austere belief in self-enlightenment, defines a level of warm and friendly spirit so unique among the Thais. Despite centuries of imperialism, Thailand has the distinction of being the only Southeast Asian country that has never been ruled by a Western power. In a sense, Thai society has stood the test of time in peace, stability, and tranquility.

Thailand bears a striking resemblance to my home country, the Philippines. People are friendly, accommodating, and hospitable beyond measure. One feels easily welcome even at first encounter.

I had my first crash program of Thai culture and its people way back in 1969 when my husband, Dr. Nikom Wannarachue, a Thai-American, brought me home to meet his family. This marked the beginning of my love affair with Thai cooking. The first taste of *Tom Yum Goong* (Spicy Shrimp Soup with Lemon Grass), the splendid touch of hot and sour with a tinge of sweetness and distinct aroma, won my taste buds at first sip. I started my incredible journey to learn more about the intricacies of Thai cuisine. Subsequent trips to Thailand became opportunities for cooking classes, not only within the confines of family and friends' kitchens, but in cooking school and restaurants as well.

Thai cuisine is unique not only in its richness and complexity, but in its universal taste, reflecting the various influences of different places. From the east, Indians brought cardamom, cinnamon, cloves, and curries. From the north came the Chinese with all sorts of noodles and the deep-frying system of cooking. The Malaysians brought *satay* or skewered meats, and Portuguese sailors brought tomatoes, potatoes, and hot peppers. Today, Thais use over 15 varieties of hot chilies – a flawless rhythm of distinctive flavor and aroma.

The Thai system of cooking is an intriguing combination of herbs and spices producing a unique flavor of spicy, sour, hot, salty-yet-sweet to the connoisseur. The textures of the various ingredients balanced with the right combination of herbs and spices, roots, fruits and leaves such as ginger, galanga, chilies, lemon grass, kaffir lime leaves, cilantro and pandan all contribute to a distinct delicate flavor at the artist's fingertip. There is no limit to the creativity of a talented chef. These herbs and spices have a way of bringing out the best in seafood, meat, or even vegetarian dishes, be they a main course, soup, or snacks. Thai people like to snack at any time of the day; it is no wonder food stalls flourish everywhere for the eager enthusiast.

As the saying goes, "know the culture of a people – know their food likewise." Thai food reflects the unquestioning independence and purity of spirit of the Thai people. The ingredients mirror their willful acceptance of the undying philosophy of Buddhism that venerates all that the environment generously offers. It is a blend of taste and aroma that embodies a Thai Buddhist's attitude towards life; warm and dignified as the Thai people, family, and monarchy.

This book on Thai cooking is my way of passing on to you what the Thai have so willingly and enthusiastically shared with me. I am sure you will love it as much as I have through the years. It is my hope that this modest publication will promote and enhance a wider and deeper level of multi-cultural awareness and understanding.

Josie Wannarachue
Kennewick, Washington
July 1998

COMPLETING THE MEAL
WITH JOSIE'S GREAT FOOD
By Coke Roth

The textures, flavors, colors, and aromas of Thai food are complex and integrated. Intriguing combinations of herbs and spices fuse to and sometimes confound the palates as to their origin, when the pure, fresh foods are dressed up and sent to town by the Master Chef, Josie Wannarachue. Some dishes display a clean citrus character, while others show an herb foundation. Sometimes, a floral perfume or a light, honey-like sweetness complements the bold heat from fresh chili peppers.

Thus, whether you select an appetizer, salad, soup or, entrée, be they meatless, exotic, or Four Star hot, the choice of an accompanying beverage with Josie's Thai food challenges the table host to new heights. The traditional food and beverage combinations we have come to know rarely deal with the unique and different sensations one experiences with Josie's unique and original recipes for Thai food.

Probably the most reliable rule to follow in picking a beverage is to drink the beverage that you like. The selection of malt beverages and wines that follows presents the reader with plenty of opportunity to select an old favorite or experiment in the spirit one accordingly exercises when selecting an item from Josie's culinary repertoire.

Beer may be the beverage of preference for those who pick the spiciest of the spicy and thus wish to douse the fire. The subtle flavor of beer may also complement a delicate dish.

The experience Josie's expert tasting panel incurred in pairing wines with foods was rather logical and straightforward. We found that dry Gewürtraminer, Semillon, and white wines such as lightly oaked Chardonnay or Dry Riesling will probably go best with mild dishes that are fragrant and citrusy. Fumé Blanc (dry Sauvignon Blanc), Semillon, or Gewürtztraminer will probably be most desirable with the dishes rich in herb flavors. Wines with a little residual sweetness, like Riesling or a Blush or Rose wine, had a tendency to quench and mitigate hotter flavors, thus complementing the richer, spicier dishes.

Red wines may also be a source of gastronomical pleasure when coupled with Thai food. The rich flavor of Josie's curries or entrees with beef, duck, or even salmon paired with the recommended red wines will be a winner.

As a final note, the wine selections we preferred come from the Pacific Northwest. Notwithstanding the fact that many of the vintners are our personal friends, the wines made in the Pacific Northwest are of world-class quality. Clearly world-class wines from all areas of the globe have applicability here. Consistent with the fact that we believe that the food at "King & I" restaurant is also world-class, we, with you, toast our friends and neighbors who make the fine wines that complement these foods. Cheers!

SPECIAL THANKS TO THAI AIRWAYS

Royal Orchid Service

2 *Vegetarian Egg Rolls*

APPETIZERS

Butterflies
Fresh Garden Rolls
Fried Tofu
Satay Beef
Satay Chicken
Stuffed Chicken Wings
Stuffed Crab
Sweet Crispy Rice Noodles
Thai Egg Rolls
Thai Fish Cakes

Butterflies

1   **package medium wonton wrappers**
1   **pound cream cheese**
1   **tablespoon dark soy sauce**
$\frac{1}{2}$ **cup imitation crab meat, chopped in small pieces**
$\frac{1}{4}$ **cup green onions, finely chopped**
2   **cups vegetable oil**

Mix cream cheese, soy sauce, crab meat, and green onions together. Spoon out a teaspoon of the mixture onto the center of each wonton wrapper. Brush sides of wrapper with water. Bring two sides together then press to seal, with the four corners out like wings. Deep-fry the butterflies in hot oil until golden brown. Let stand to drain oil. Serve with Spring Roll Sauce (*see recipe on page 148*). Serves four.

Wine Recommendations:

Johannesburg Riesling

Fresh Garden Rolls

8	prawns, shelled, deveined and steamed
$\frac{1}{2}$	cup pineapple tidbits
8	fresh mint tops
1	small cucumber, thinly sliced
1	cup white rice noodles, boiled for one minute
1	cup lettuce, shredded
$\frac{1}{2}$	cup carrots, shredded
8	rice paper wrappers
	cilantro leaves for garnish

Combine first 7 ingredients. Set aside. Dip each rice paper wrapper for 20 seconds in a large bowl of hot water. Place on a flat surface. Roll 2 tablespoons of the filling in the rice paper wrapper. Fold the ends well and roll up the rice paper completely. Serve with Spring Roll Sauce or cut into 3 pieces and top with Peanut Sauce *(see recipe on page 147)*. *See picture on page 124.* Serves four.

Wine Recommendations:

Fruity Sauvignon Blanc

5

Fried Tofu

1   8-ounce package fresh, firm tofu, Chinese
2   cups vegetable oil

Sauce:
4   tablespoons white vinegar
4   tablespoons sugar
1   teaspoon salt
½   teaspoon chili powder or 1 fresh red chili
2   tablespoons ground roasted peanuts

Slice tofu in half lengthwise. Deep-fry for 3-5 minutes, or until golden-brown Drain, slice into bite-sized pieces, and arrange on a platter. In a saucepan, heat ingredients for the sauce, stirring until thoroughly mixed. Pour into a bowl and serve with tofu. Garnish sauce with cilantro leaves. Serves four.

Wine Recommendations:

Champagne
Fruity Semillon
Sauvignon Blanc

Fried Tofu

Satay Beef

1   cup coconut milk
2   tablespoons cilantro leaves
1   tablespoon sugar
1   tablespoon yellow curry powder
4   tablespoons fish sauce
1   tablespoon olive oil
2   cups beef, cut in strips about 3 inches long
bamboo skewers

In a large bowl, marinate beef strips with the first 6 ingredients for 1 hour. Thread pieces of meat on bamboo skewers. Broil, grill, or pan-fry for 5 minutes. Serve with Peanut Sauce (*see recipe on page 147*) and Cucumber Salad. Serves four.

Wine Recommendations:

Chardonnay

Satay Chicken

1	cup coconut milk
2	tablespoons cilantro leaves
1	tablespoon sugar
1	tablespoon yellow curry powder
4	tablespoons fish sauce
1	tablespoon olive oil
2	cups chicken breast, cut in strips about 3 inches long

bamboo skewers

In a large bowl, marinate chicken strips with the first 6 ingredients for 1 hour. Thread pieces of meat on bamboo skewers. Broil, grill, or pan-fry for 5 minutes. Serve with Peanut Sauce (*see recipe on page 147*) and Cucumber Salad. Serves four.

Wine Recommendations:

Chardonnay

Stuffed Chicken Wings

2   pounds drummettes, deboned
1   package cellophane noodles, soaked in hot water for 3 minutes, drained
1   pound medium shrimp, shelled and deveined
1   carrot, shredded
1   cup water chestnuts, finely chopped
¼   cup green onion, finely chopped
4   cloves garlic
2   tablespoons fish sauce
1   tablespoon fresh cilantro, finely chopped
1   teaspoon ground white pepper
1   cup rice flour
3   cups vegetable oil for deep-frying

Debone chicken drummettes. Set aside. Cut the cellophane noodles into 1-inch lengths. In a food processor, chop the chicken and shrimp. In a bowl, combine all ingredients and mix thoroughly. Stuff the mixture into the drummettes and coat drummettes with rice flour. Using a wok, deep-fry over medium heat for about 3 minutes on each side or until golden brown. Serve with Hot Chili Sweet Sauce (*see recipe on page 144*). Serves four.

Wine Recommendations:

Gewürtztraminer

10

Stuffed Crab

5	large crabs, steamed
1	cup dried black mushrooms, soaked in water and thinly sliced
1	cup small shrimps, shelled
1	onion, chopped
1	carrot, chopped
½	cup water chestnuts, chopped
2	eggs
1	tablespoon cornstarch
2	tablespoons garlic salt
1	teaspoon ground black pepper
½	cup green onion, thinly sliced
½	cup cilantro, thinly sliced vegetable oil for deep frying

Remove crabmeat from the shells and set shells aside. Finely chop crabmeat and shrimp. Combine crabmeat with the rest of the ingredients. Stuff the shells with the crabmeat mixture. Deep fry shells over medium heat for 12 to 15 minutes or until golden brown and set aside to drain. Arrange crabs over a bed of lettuce leaves. Serve with Hot Chili Sweet Sauce (*see recipe on page 144*). Serves four.

Wine Recommendations:

Chardonnay
Semillon

Sweet Crispy Rice Noodles

1	package fine thin rice noodles
1/4	cup finely chopped fresh shrimp
1/4	cup finely chopped pork
1	fried tofu, cut into small pieces
1	cup bean sprouts
2	tablespoons cilantro leaves
1	finely sliced spur chili
1	tablespoon chopped garlic and shallots
2	pickled garlic bulbs, finely sliced
1	teaspoon ground dried chilies
4	teaspoons sugar
1	tablespoon vinegar
3	cups vegetable oil for frying
2	tablespoons lemon juice
	bean sprouts for garnish

Fry noodles in oil until crisp and golden. Drain. Heat 1/4 cup oil in a frying pan. Fry garlic and shallots until fragrant. Add the pork, shrimp, seasoning with vinegar, fish sauce, sugar, and ground dried chilies. When thick, add lemon juice, mix and season to obtain sweet, sour, and salty flavor. Reduce the heat, add noodles and continue turning them until they stick together, add the bean curd. Transfer onto plates. Sprinkle with the pickled garlic, finely sliced lemon rind, cilantro, and red spur chili. Garnish with bean sprouts on sides of the plates. Serves four.

Wine Recommendations:

Gewürtztraminer
Johannesburg Reisling

Sweet Crispy Rice Noodles   **13**

Thai Egg Rolls

1	package spring roll sheets
1	cup ground pork
1	cup ground beef
2	eggs
2	cups mung bean noodles
1	cup finely sliced cabbage
1	cup sliced carrots
1	cup bean sprouts
1	cup onions
1	tablespoon chopped garlic
1	cup wheat flour paste (5 tablespoons wheat flour in 1 cup water stirred over low heat)
1	teaspoon ground pepper
2	tablespoons garlic salt
2	tablespoons light soy sauce
	fresh fruit for garnish

Soak noodles until soft, then cut into 2-inch lengths. Mix pork, eggs, beef, cabbage, carrots, bean sprouts, garlic salt, light soy sauce, and noodles together. Brown the garlic and then add the pork, beef, and noodle mixture. Cook for 5 minutes. Strain. Place a tablespoon of filling on a spring roll sheet. Fold 3 ends together, then roll up completely and seal with wheat flour paste. Deep fry over medium heat until crisp and golden brown. Serve with Spring Roll Sauce (*see recipe on page 148*). Garnish with fresh fruit. Serves four.

Note: For vegetarian egg rolls, omit pork and beef and roll mixture without folding end. *See picture on page 2.*

Wine Recommendctions:
  Fumé Rosé

14

Thai Egg Rolls

15

Thai Fish Cakes

4	cups white fish meat, chopped
2	eggs
$\frac{1}{2}$	cup string beans, sliced fine
3	tablespoons kaffir lime leaves, chopped
1	teaspoon sugar
1	teaspoon salt
1	tablespoon red curry paste
3	cups vegetable oil for frying

Put all ingredients, except the string beans in a food processor and blend until paste consistency is achieved, then add string beans and mix well. Shape the mixture into patties 2 inches in diameter and ½ inch thick. Deep-fry until golden brown. Serve with Hot Chili Sweet Sauce (*see recipe on page 144*). Serves four.

Wine Recommendations:

Gamay Beaujolais

Thai Fish Cakes **17**

18   *Mangosteen Fruits*

SOUPS

Chicken Coconut Milk Soup
Prawn Coconut Milk Soup
Rice Soup
Silver Noodle Soup
Spicy and Sour Seafood Soup
Spicy Shrimp Soup with Lemon Grass
Thai Chicken Soup with Bean Threads
Thai Ginger Chicken Soup
Thai Noodle Soup with Chicken
Thai Noodle Soup with Pork Meatballs
Three is Company Soup

Chicken Coconut Milk Soup

1	cup chicken breast, sliced
2	cups coconut milk
1	cup chicken stock
10	slices of galanga
10	slices of lemon grass, lower portion only
6	kaffir lime leaves, cut in half
4	tablespoons fish sauce
4	pieces baby corn, cut in half
1	tablespoon sugar
½	cup fresh lime juice
1	tablespoon sour paste
2	red chilis, crushed
4	fresh mushrooms, sliced thinly
1	tomato
	cilantro and green onions for garnish

Combine stock with galanga, lemon grass and lime leaves in a large saucepan and bring to boil. Add chicken, fish sauce, sugar, and half of the coconut milk. Cook until chicken is done, then add remaining ingredients. Continue cooking till mixture is boiling. Pour soup into a serving bowl and garnish with cilantro and green onions. Serves four.

Chicken Coconut Milk Soup　　**21**

Prawn Coconut Milk Soup

10	prawns, shelled and deveined
2	cups coconut milk
1	cup chicken stock
10	slices of galanga
10	slices of lemon grass, lower portion only
6	kaffir lime leaves, cut in half
4	tablespoons fish sauce
4	pieces baby corn, cut in half
1	tablespoon sugar
¼	cup fresh lime juice
1	tablespoon sour paste
2	red chilis, crushed
4	fresh mushrooms, sliced thinly
1	tomato
	cilantro and green onions for garnish

Combine stock with galanga, lemon grass and lime leaves in a large saucepan and bring to boil. Add prawns, fish sauce, sugar and half of the coconut milk. Cook until prawns are done. Add all remaining ingredients and continue cooking till mixture is boiling. Pour soup into a serving bowl and garnish with cilantro and green onions. Serves four.

Prawn Coconut Milk Soup **23**

Rice Soup

5 cups chicken stock
¼ cup minced beef, chicken, pork, fish, or shrimp
1 tablespoon minced common ginger
2½ cups cooked rice
1-2 tablespoons fish sauce
1 egg
green onions, cilantro, onion flakes and red chili flakes for garnish

In a stockpot, heat chicken stock. Add minced meat or seafood and ginger; bring to a boil, stirring occasionally. Reduce heat to simmer. Add rice and cook for 2 minutes. Season with fish sauce. In a serving bowl, beat egg lightly. Pour soup on top of the egg. Garnish with green onions, onion flakes, and red chili flakes. Serve hot. Serves four.

Silver Noodle Soup

1	cup ground pork
3	tablespoons fish sauce
1	tablespoon Maggi sauce or plain soy sauce
1	tablespoon white pepper
5	white peppercorns, crushed
5	cups chicken stock
3	garlic cloves, crushed
1	8-ounce package of silver noodles (or cellophane or glass), soaked in water
1	cup cabbage, sliced
½	cup sliced carrot
2	green onions, cut into half-inch pieces
	cilantro for garnish

Mix pork, soy sauce, and white pepper well. Form into small meatballs and set aside. Heat the stock, add the crushed garlic and peppercorns and bring to a boil. Place meatballs in boiling stock. Add the noodles. Cook until meatballs are done. Add remaining ingredients and cook for 2 minutes. Remove from heat immediately. Pour soup into a tureen and garnish with cilantro. Serves four.

Spicy and Sour Seafood Soup

2	tablespoons lemongrass, sliced thinly
2	tablespoons cilantro
2	cloves garlic, minced
3	fresh chilies, seeded
5	kaffir lime leaves, chopped
5	cups chicken stock
6	shelled prawns, deveined
½	cup squid, cut into small pieces
½	cup fish fillet, cut into small pieces
2	mussels
1	cup fresh mushrooms, sliced
2	tablespoons water chestnuts
5	tablespoons lime juice
2	tablespoons fish sauce
2	tomatoes, sliced
	cilantro and green onion for garnish

In a large saucepan, combine lemongrass, cilantro, garlic, chili, kaffir and lime to form a paste. In a separate pot, bring chicken stock to a boil and add mushrooms and water chestnuts to it. Add the seafood and cook for another 2-3 minutes longer. Pour the mixture into a soup tureen and garnish with cilantro and green onions. Serves four.

Spicy and Sour Seafood Soup　　**27**

Spicy Shrimp Soup with Lemon Grass

8	prawns, shelled and deveined
4	cups water
1	stalk fresh lemon grass, sliced
1	can straw mushrooms, drained (8 ounces)
2	kaffir lime leaves
1-4	tablespoons fish sauce
¼	cup fresh lime juice
2	tablespoons sliced green onions
1	tablespoon chopped cilantro
1-4	red chili peppers, seeded and chopped or ½ teaspoon red chili paste

Bring water to a boil. Add lemon grass and straw mushrooms, immediately reducing heat to medium low. Add shrimp and cook for 3 minutes. Stir in the fish sauce and lime juice. Sprinkle with green onions, cilantro and red chili peppers if desired. Serve hot. Serves four.

Thai Chicken Soup with Bean Threads

5	cups chicken stock
1	cup bean threads, soaked and drained
1	cup boneless chicken breast, thinly sliced
½	cup straw mushrooms, drained
½	cup miniature corn, drained
½	cup water chestnuts, thinly sliced
¼	cup shredded bamboo shoots
2	stalks green onions, cut into 2-inch lengths
	cilantro for garnish

Add all ingredients to boiling chicken stock. Reduce heat and simmer for 3 to 5 minutes. Garnish with cilantro. Serves four.

Thai Ginger Chicken Soup

½	pound boneless chicken breast
3	cups coconut milk
2	cups water
1	1-inch section ginger, thinly sliced
1-4	tablespoons fish sauce
¼	cup fresh lime juice
	cilantro and green onions for garnish

Cut chicken into thin strips. Bring coconut milk and water to a boil. Reduce heat to medium low. Add chicken and cook for 3 minutes. Stir in the ginger, fish sauce and lime juice. Sprinkle with green onions and cilantro. Serve hot. Serves four.

Thai Noodle Soup with Chicken

¼   pound rice noodles
5   cups chicken stock
½   pound boneless chicken breast, finely chopped
½   cup bean sprouts
1-2 teaspoons fish sauce
     cilantro, green onions, and red chili peppers for garnish

Soak rice noodles in warm water for 15 minutes. Drain. Bring the soup stock to a boil. Add rice noodles, chicken, and bean sprouts. Season with fish sauce. Reduce heat and simmer for 5 to 7 minutes. Garnish with cilantro, green onions and red chili peppers. Serves four.

Thai Noodle Soup with Pork Meatballs

¼   pound rice noodles
5   cups chicken stock
½   pound pork meatballs or shredded pork
½   cup fresh bean sprouts
1-2 teaspoons fish sauce
1   Thai broccoli, julienned
     cilantro, green onions, and red chilies for garnish

Soak rice noodles in warm water for 15 minutes. Drain. Bring soup stock to a boil. Add meatballs and cook for 3 minutes. Add remaining ingredients and cook for another 3 minutes. Garnish with cilantro, green onions and red chilies. Serves four.

Thai Noodle Soup with Pork Meatballs **31**

Three is Company Soup

½   cup chicken, thinly sliced
½   cup fish, sliced
5   cups chicken stock
1   Chinese radish, peeled and cut into 1-inch peices
1   cup spinach
4   prawns, shelled and deveined
2   tablespoons fish sauce
1   teaspoon red pepper powder
    cilantro and green onion for garnish

Heat soup stock, add chicken and cook for 2 minutes. Add reaming ingredients and cook for 3 minutes. Sprinkle with green onion and cilantro. Serve immediately. Serves four.

Three is Company Soup 33

Thai Orchids

SALADS

Bean Sprout Prawns
Calamari Salad with Fresh Lemon Grass
Chiang Mai Chicken Salad
Green Papaya Salad
Special Eggplant Salad
Spicy Mung Bean Noodle Salad
Spicy and Sour Seafood Salad
Thai Beef Salad
Thai Eggplant Salad
Thai Pomelo or Grapefruit Salad
Thai Prawn Salad

Bean Sprout Prawns

3	tablespoons olive oil
1	tablespoon garlic, minced or chopped
8	prawns, shelled and deveined
3	tablespoons fish sauce
1	pound fresh bean sprouts
1	teaspoon sugar
$\frac{1}{2}$	teaspoon white pepper
	lettuce leaves
	cilantro and green onions for garnish

Brown the garlic in oil, then add prawns. When prawns are cooked, add remaining ingredients and stir fry for 1 minute. Garnish with green onions and cilantro. Serve over a bed of green lettuce. Serves four.

Wine Recommendations:

Fumé Rosé

Calamari Salad with Fresh Lemon Grass

½   cup water
1   pound calamari (squid), cut into small pieces
1   stalk fresh lemon grass, finely chopped
3   fresh kaffir lime leaves, finely chopped
1   onion, thinly sliced
5   teaspoons fresh lime juice
1   tablespoon fish sauce
3   red chili peppers, seeded and chopped
10   mint leaves
5   sprigs Chinese parsley, chopped
1   green onion, finely chopped

In a small saucepan, bring water to a boil and add calamari. Cook for 3-5 minutes or until opaque. Drain. Set aside to cool. In a big mixing bowl, combine remaining ingredients. Add calamari. Mix well. Serve chilled or near room temperature. Serves four.

Wine Recommendations:

Chardonnay

Chiang Mai Chicken Salad

1   pound boneless chicken, ground
1   stalk fresh lemon grass, finely chopped
3   kaffir lime leaves, finely chopped
3-6 red chili peppers, seeded and chopped (optional)
¼   cup fresh lime juice
1-2 tablespoons fish sauce
1   green onion, chopped
6-8 sprigs cilantro
12   mint leaves, chopped
1   teaspoon ground red chili peppers (optional)
     green onions and cilantro for garnish

In a small skillet, cook chicken with a ½ cup of water. Drain and set the chicken aside to cool. Mix the chicken with lemon grass, kaffir lime leaves, chopped red chili peppers, lime juice and fish sauce. Stir in the green onion, cilantro, and chopped mint leaves and add to the chicken. Transfer to a platter and serve with lettuce leaves. Garnish with green onions and mint leaves. Serves four.

Wine Recommendations:

Chardonnay

Chiang Mai Chicken Salad **39**

Green Papaya Salad

4	cloves garlic
4	chilies
2	cups green papaya, shredded or grated
1	tablespoon dried shrimp
1	large tomato, cut into wedges
2	tablespoons fish sauce
4	tablespoons lime juice
1	tablespoon brown or white sugar
	roasted and shelled peanuts for garnish

Crush garlic cloves and chilies. Mix all ingredients together. Place into a salad dish and sprinkle roasted peanuts on top. Serves four.

Note: Carrots or cucumbers may be used instead of green papaya.

Wine Recommendations:

Gewürtztraminer

Green Papaya Salad   **41**

Special Eggplant Salad

2	eggplants, thinly sliced diagonally
1	small onion, thinly sliced
1	small cucumber, thinly sliced
2	cilantro sprigs
2	green onions, finely sliced
1	small carrot, finely sliced

Dressing:

3	tablespoons fish sauce
¼	cup lime juice
2	tablespoons sugar
1	teaspoon sriracha sauce

Combine ingredients for the dressing and set aside. Grill eggplant slices until soft. Mix all ingredients with the eggplant. Pour the dressing over the salad. Toss lightly and serve. Serves four.

Wine Recommendations:

Gewürtztraminer

Spicy Mung Bean Noodle Salad

2   cups mung bean noodles, cut into 2-inch lengths
½   cup pork, cut into thin slices and steamed
½   cup pork liver, cut into thin slices and steamed
      (optional)
½   cup prawns, cut into thin slices and boiled
½   cup spring shallots, thinly sliced
½   cup cilantro, cut into 1-inch lengths
1   head green lettuce

Dressing:
3   hot chilies
1   teaspoon pickled garlic, thinly sliced
1   tablespoon cilantro root, thinly sliced
½   cup sugar
1   teaspoon salt
½   cup vinegar

Combine all ingredients in a large bowl. Add dressing and toss gently. Place salad on a bed of lettuce. Serves four.

Wine Recommendations:

Gamay Beaujolais
Merlot

44   *Spicy and Sour Seafood Salad*

Spicy and Sour Seafood Salad

4	tiger prawns, shelled, deveined, and steamed
½	cup calamari, steamed and cut into small pieces with a criss-cross pattern cut on them
4	mussels on half-shells, steamed
½	cup fish balls or fish fillet, steamed
½	cup cilantro, cut into 1-inch lengths
2	shallots, cut into thin slices
1	head lettuce

Dressing:

2	red spur chilies, well crushed
5	garlic cloves, well crushed
1	teaspoon sugar
5	tablespoons lime juice
5	tablespoons fish sauce

Combine ingredients for the dressing. Place prawns, calamari, mussels, fish balls, cilantro, and shallot in a bowl. Add the dressing and toss gently. Wash lettuce, cut into pieces and arrange on a platter. Spoon the salad onto the lettuce and serve. Serves four.

Wine Recommendations:

Gewürtztraminer

Thai Beef Salad

1	tablespoon garlic, crushed
10	small chilies, cut in half
3	tablespoons fish sauce
3	tablespoons lime juice
1	tablespoon sugar
1	green onion
1	cucumber, sliced thinly
2	heads lettuce
2	cups sirloin steak, grilled rare and sliced thinly cilantro, mint and sliced chilies for garnish

Mix ingredients together and toss with the sliced steak. Place salad on a bed of lettuce on a serving platter and garnish with cilantro, mint, and sliced chilies. Serves four.

Wine Recommendations:

Merlot

Thai Eggplant Salad

2   long eggplants
¼   cup ground pork, steamed
4   prawns, shelled, deveined, and steamed
2   tablespoons mint leaves

Dressing:
4   hot chilies, sliced
3   tablespoons shallots, sliced
3   tablespoons fish sauce
5   tablespoons lime juice
1   tablespoon sugar

Combine ingredients for the dressing. Grill eggplants until soft. Peel eggplants, and then slice into sections. Add prawns and pork to the eggplants, then add the dressing and toss gently to mix. Transfer to a salad bowl, sprinkle with mint leaves and serve. Serves four.

Wine Recommendations:

Gamay Beaujolais

47

Thai Pomelo or Grapefruit Salad

2	large pomelos or grapefruits
2	tablespoons fresh lime juice
2	tablespoons fish sauce
1	cup dried shrimp
3	tablespoons sweetened coconut flakes or fresh grated coconut
½	cup coconut milk

Peel and section pomelos. Set aside. In a salad bowl, mix 5 remaining ingredients well. Add pomelos and toss well. Serves four.

Wine Recommendations:

Fumé Rosé

Thai Prawn Salad

12 prawns, shelled, deveined, and steamed
1 small onion, thinly sliced
4 tablespoons carrots, grated
3 red chilies, thinly sliced
½ cup cucumbers, thinly sliced
1 head green lettuce
green onions, cilantro and mint leaves for garnish

Dressing:
1 teaspoon sriracha sauce
3 tablespoons fish sauce
4 tablespoons fresh lime juice
1 tablespoon brown sugar

Toss salad ingredients. Arrange salad over a bed of lettuce leaves. Mix dressing and pour over salad. Garnish with green onions, cilantro and mint leaves. Serves four.

Note: Palm sugar may be substituted for brown sugar.

Wine Recommendations:

Chardonnay,

49

DEAN

50 *Chiang-Rai*

RICE AND NOODLES

Fried Rice with Pork
Pineapple Fried Rice
Prawn Fried Rice
Seafood Fried Rice
Spicy Pork Fried Rice with Basil
Tofu Fried Rice
Seafood over Spicy Noodles
Stir-Fried Thai Noodles
Thai Broccoli Noodles with Chicken
Yellow Noodles with Pork
Yellow Noodles with Prawns

Fried Rice with Pork

4	tablespoons vegetable oil
2	tablespoons garlic, chopped
½	cup onion
1	cup pork, thinly sliced and marinated in soy sauce
2	cups cooked rice
3	tablespoons light soy sauce
2	tablespoons catsup
5	spring onions
2	eggs, slightly beaten
	cucumbers, green mango, and Chinese sausage for garnish

Brown the garlic in oil, then add onion and pork. Cook until meat is done. Add the cooked rice and remaining ingredients to the meat. Mix thoroughly until well blended. In a separate pan, cook the eggs. Cut into small pieces. Add eggs to fried rice. Garnish with onions, chili, cucumbers, green sliced mango and Chinese sausage. Serves four.

Wine Recommendations:

Chardonnay
Enjoy the wine – most wines will go well with this dish

Fried Rice with Pork **53**

Pineapple Fried Rice

2	tablespoons olive oil
1	tablespoon chopped garlic
¼	cup onion, chopped
½	cup chicken, julienne cut
1	cup pineapple cubes
3	cups cooked rice
2	tablespoons chopped carrots
2	tablespoons green peas
2	tablespoons soy sauce
1	tablespoon fish sauce
2	tablespoons oyster sauce
	cucumber, tomatoes and pineapple slices for garnish

Brown the garlic in oil. Add onions and chicken, cooking until chicken is done. Add rice, followed by remaining ingredients. Mix well, cooking for 3-5 minutes. Garnish with pineapple, tomato and cucumber. Serves four.

Wine Recommendations:

Pinot Gris

Pineapple Fried Rice   **55**

Prawn Fried Rice

2	tablespoons vegetable oil
1	tablespoon garlic, chopped
½	cup onion, diced
8	prawns, shelled and deveined
3	cups cooked rice
2	tablespoons chopped carrots
2	tablespoons green peas
2	tablespoons soy sauce
1	tablespoon fish sauce
2	tablespoons oyster sauce
	cilantro for garnish

Brown the garlic in oil. Add onions and prawns. Add rice, followed by remaining ingredients. Mix well, cooking for 3 minutes. Garnish with cilantro. Serves four.

Wine Recommendations:

Reisling

Seafood Fried Rice

2	tablespoons vegetable oil
1	tablespoon garlic, chopped
½	cup onion, diced
4	mussels, in half-shells
4	prawns, peeled and deveined
½	cup calamari, cut diagonally with a criss-cross pattern cut into pieces
4	small slices of fish fillet
3	cups cooked rice
2	tablespoons chopped carrots
2	tablespoons green peas
2	tablespoons soy sauce
1	tablespoon fish sauce
2	tablespoons oyster sauce

Brown the garlic in oil. Add onions, mussels, prawns, calamari, and fish, cooking until the seafood is done. Add rice, followed by remaining ingredients. Mix well, cooking for 3 minutes. Garnish with cilantro. Serves four.

Wine Recommendations:

Dry Reisling
Light Sauvignon Blanc

Spicy Pork Fried Rice with Basil

½	cup vegetable oil (for frying the basil leaves)
½	cup basil leaves
3	tablespoons cooking oil
2	tablespoons garlic, chopped
½	cup onion, chopped
1	cup ground pork
3	cups cooked rice
2	red chilies, cut in half
2	green chilies, cut in half
2	yellow chilies, cut in half
1	tablespoon garlic
2	tablespoons fish sauce

Heat ½ cup oil and fry basil leaves until crisp. Remove from oil and set aside to drain. With the 3 tablespoons oil, brown the garlic in a separate pan, then add onions and pork. Cook pork until done. Add the remainder of the ingredients and cook for 3 minutes. Mix basil leaves into the fried rice and serve. Serves four.

Wine Recommendations:

Gewürtztraminer

Tofu Fried Rice

2	tablespoons vegetable oil
1	tablespoon garlic, chopped
¼	cup onion, diced
1	cup tofu, cut into strips
3	cups cooked rice
2	tablespoons chopped carrots
2	tablespoons green peas
2	tablespoons soy sauce
1	tablespoons fish sauce
2	tablespoons oyster sauce
	cilantro for garnish

Brown the garlic in oil. Add tofu and onions. Cook until tofu is done. Add rice, followed by the remaining ingredients. Mix well, cooking for 3 minutes. Garnish with cilantro. Serves four.

Wine Recommendations:

Sauvignon Blanc

Seafood over Spicy Noodles

4	tablespoons vegetable oil
2	cups inch-wide rice noodles, soaked
2	tablespoons garlic, chopped
$\frac{1}{2}$	cup calamari, cut with a criss-cross pattern
$\frac{1}{2}$	cup scallops
4	prawns, shelled and deveined
$\frac{1}{2}$	cup Chinese broccoli
1	cup carrots, julienne cut
1	tablespoon oyster sauce
1	tablespoon sugar
1	tablespoon soy sauce
1	cup soup stock or water

Heat 3 tablespoons oil and stir fry the noodles until done. Set aside on a platter. Brown the garlic in the remaining oil and add seafood. Stir fry for 3 minutes, then add remaining ingredients. Stir fry for another 2 minutes. Mix with noodles and serve. Serves four.

Wine Recommendations:

Chardonnay
Sauvignon Blanc

Seafood on Spicy Noodles **61**

Stir Fried Thai Noodles

Stir Fried Thai Noodles

1	pack rice noodles, soaked in water for 1 hour
3	tablespoons vegetable oil
1	tablespoon garlic, chopped
3	tablespoons sugar
3	tablespoons lime juice
1	tablespoon paprika
2	tablespoons fish sauce
2	tablespoons dark soy sauce
1	cup fried tofu, cut into small pieces
2	eggs, beaten
1	cup chicken, sliced thinly
3	tablespoons unsalted peanuts, chopped and shelled
1	cup fresh bean sprouts
2	spring onions, cut into 1-inch lengths
3	steamed prawns, shelled and deveined
	lime wedges for garnish

Brown the garlic in oil. Add chicken and cook until done. Add rice noodles and stir over high heat for 3 minutes until noodles are soft. Add sugar, lime juice, paprika, fish sauce, soy sauce, and eggs, and cook for 1 minute. Add tofu, peanuts, and spring onions and continue mixing for another minute. Turn off heat and add fresh bean sprouts. Garnish with fresh vegetables and lime wedges. Top with the prawns. Serve immediately. Serves four.

Note: Tamarind sauce can be substituted for lime juice.

Wine Recommendations:
Gewürtztraminer
Light Body Semillon

Thai Broccoli Noodles with Chicken

6 tablespoons vegetable oil
½ pound fresh wide rice noodles (if not fresh, soak the noodles in water for 1 hour)
2 eggs, beaten
2 tablespoons garlic, finely chopped
¼ pound chicken breast, sliced thinly
1 pound broccoli, julienned thinly
1 carrot, julienned
2 tablespoons cornstarch, dissolved in 4 tablespoons water
3 tablespoons yellow bean sauce
3 tablespoons oyster sauce

In 2 tablespoons oil, cook rice noodles and eggs for 2 minutes on medium heat. Place mixture on a large serving platter and set aside. Brown the garlic in the remaining oil. Add chicken and cook for 2 minutes. Add remaining ingredients and stir fry for 4-5 minutes. Pour mixture over the noodles. Toss lightly and serve immediately. Serves four.

Wine Recommendations:

Fruity Merlot

Broccoli Noodles with Chicken **65**

Yellow Noodles with Pork

3	tablespoons vegetable oil
2	tablespoons garlic, chopped
½	cup onion, chopped
1	cup pork, cut into strips
4	cups yellow noodles, steamed if fresh. (If packaged, oil the noodles until soft, then drain and set aside.)
2	tablespoons fish sauce
3	tablespoons oyster sauce
2	tablespoons chives, cut into 2 inch lengths
1	cup chopped cabbage
1	cup chopped carrots
	cilantro for garnish

Brown the garlic in oil. Add onion and pork. Cook until pork is done. Add cabbage and carrots and stir fry for 2 minutes. Add noodles and remaining ingredients. Mix well and cook for 5 minutes. Garnish with cilantro. Serves four.

Wine Recommendations:

Syrah

Yellow Noodles with Prawns

2	tablespoons chives, cut into 2-inch lengths
1	cup chopped cabbage
1	cup chopped carrots
4	cups yellow noodles, steamed if fresh. (If packaged, boil the noodles until soft, then drain and set side.)
2	tablespoons fish sauce
3	tablespoons oyster sauce
3	tablespoons vegetable oil
2	tablespoons garlic, chopped
$\frac{1}{2}$	cup onion, chopped
8	steamed prawns, shelled and deveined
	cilantro for garnish

Brown the garlic in oil. Add onion and the remaining ingredients, except for the prawns. Mix well and cook for 5 minutes. Add prawns and garnish with cilantro. Serves four.

Wine Recommendations:

Sauvignon Blanc

67

Varieties of Chilies

CURRIES

Chicken Green Curry
Chicken Yellow Curry
Green Chicken Curry
Mussamun Beef Curry
Panang Beef Curry
Panang Chicken Curry
Panang Duck Curry
Pineapple Curry with Prawns
Red Curry Prawns
Red Pork Curry
Roast Duck Curry
Steamed Pork, Fish & Chicken Curry
Thai Crab Curry

Chicken Green Curry

1	tablespoon vegetable oil
3	tablespoons green curry paste
3	cups coconut milk
1	cup chicken breast, thinly sliced
1	cup eggplant, cut into bite-sized pieces
5	sprigs basil
2	kaffir lime leaves, finely sliced
	red chili sliced lengthwise for garnish

Heat the oil and stir fry the green curry paste for 3 minutes. Add coconut milk to the curry paste and let boil over medium heat. Add chicken and cook until done. Add remaining ingredients and cook for 5 minutes. Garnish with red chili. Serves four.

Wine Recommendations:

Merlot

Chicken Green Curry

Chicken Yellow Curry

1	tablespoon vegetable oil
3	tablespoons yellow curry paste
3	cups coconut milk
1	cup chicken breast, thinly sliced
4	tablespoons green peas
½	cup red and green bell peppers, sliced
3	tablespoons fish sauce

Heat oil and stir fry yellow curry paste for 3 minutes. Add coconut milk to the curry paste and bring to a boil over medium heat. Then add chicken and cook until done. Add remaining ingredients and cook for 5 minutes. Serves four.

Wine Recommendations:

Dry Reisling
Zinfandel

Green Prawn Curry

1	tablespoon vegetable oil
3	tablespoons green curry paste
3	cups coconut milk
1	cup Thai green eggplant, cut into small pieces
8	prawns, shelled and deveined
3	kaffir lime leaves, cut in half
1	stalk fresh lemon grass, thinly sliced
5	sprigs basil
3	tablespoons fish sauce
3	small green chili peppers, seeded and chopped (optional)

Heat oil and stir fry green curry paste for 3 minutes. Add coconut milk to the curry paste and bring to a boil over medium heat. Add eggplant and cook for 3 minutes. Add remaining ingredients and cook for 5 minutes. Serves four.

Wine Recommendations:

Dry Reisling
Merlot

Mussamun Beef Curry

1	tablespoon olive oil
3	tablespoons mussamun chili paste
3	cups coconut milk
1	cup beef, thinly sliced
5	peeled small onions
5	small potatoes, peeled and boiled
2	tablespoons roasted peanuts
3	bay leaves
5	roasted cardamon fruits
1	piece of roasted cinnamon, pounded
3	tablespoons tamarind juice or lime juice
3	tablespoons fish sauce

Heat the oil and stir fry the mussamun chili paste for 3 minutes. Add coconut milk to the chili paste and bring to a boil over medium heat. Add beef and let simmer for 5 minutes, or until the beef is tender. Add remainder of ingredients and let simmer for another 5 minutes. Taste and adjust the flavor till it is sweet, salty, and sour. Serves four.

Wine Recommendations:

Cabernet Sauvignon

Panang Beef Curry

1	tablespoon vegetable oil
3	tablespoons panang curry paste
3	cups coconut milk
2	cups beef, cut into thin strips
4	tablespoons roasted peanuts
1	tablespoon sugar
3	tablespoons fish sauce
$\frac{1}{2}$	cup red and green bell peppers, sliced
5	kaffir lime leaves, cut into pieces
5	sprigs basil

Heat oil and stir fry panang curry paste for 3 minutes. Add coconut milk to the curry paste. Bring to a boil over medium heat. Add beef and cook for 5 minutes, or until beef is done. Add the roasted peanuts, sugar, fish sauce and green bell peppers. Let simmer for 8-10 minutes, stirring occasionally. Add kaffir and basil. Remove from heat. Serves four.

Wine Recommendations:

Fruity Merlot
Semillon

75

Panang Chicken Curry

Panang Chicken Curry

1	tablespoon vegetable oil
3	tablespoons panang curry paste
3	cups coconut milk
2	cups chicken breast, thinly sliced
4	tablespoons roasted peanuts
1	tablespoon sugar
3	tablespoons fish sauce
$\frac{1}{2}$	cup red and green bell peppers, sliced
5	kaffir lime leaves, cut into pieces
5	sprigs basil

Heat oil and stir fry panang curry paste for 3 minutes. Add coconut milk to the curry paste. Bring to a boil over medium heat. Add chicken and cook for 5 minutes, or until chicken is done. Add the roasted peanuts, sugar, fish sauce and green bell peppers. Let simmer for 8-10 minutes, stirring occasionally. Add kaffir and basil. Remove from heat and serve with rice. Serves four.

Wine Recommendations:

Dry Reisling
Semillon

Panang Duck Curry

1	tablespoon vegetable oil
3	tablespoons panang curry paste
3	cups coconut milk
2	cups roast duck, sliced and deboned
4	tablespoons roasted peanuts
1	tablespoon sugar
3	tablespoons fish sauce
½	cup red and green bell peppers, sliced
5	kaffir lime leaves, cut into pieces
5	sprigs basil

Heat oil and stir fry panang curry paste until fragrant. Add coconut milk and bring to a boil. Add remaining ingredients, except for kaffir and basil and let simmer for 8-10 minutes on medium heat. Add kaffir and basil and then remove the curry from heat and serve. Serves four.

Wine Recommendations:

Zinfandel

Pineapple Curry with Prawns

1	tablespoon vegetable oil
3	tablespoons red chili paste
3	cups coconut milk
1	cup pineapple, chopped
1	small red bell pepper, sliced
2	kaffir lime leaves, torn into pieces
2	tablespoons tamarind or lime juice
2	tablespoons fish sauce
2	tablespoons green peas
8	prawns, shelled and deveined

Heat oil and stir fry red chili paste until fragrant. Add coconut milk and bring to a boil over medium heat. Cook for 3 minutes. Add the next 6 ingredients and cook for another 5 minutes. Add prawns and cook for one more minute. Remove from heat and serve. Serves four.

Wine Recommendations:

Sauvignon Blanc

79

Red Curry Prawns

1	tablespoon vegetable oil
3	tablespoons red curry paste
3	cups coconut milk
1	cup straw mushrooms, sliced in half
$\frac{1}{2}$	cup green and red bell peppers, sliced
5	sprigs basil
1	teaspoon sugar
2	tablespoons fish sauce
8	prawns, shelled and deveined

Heat oil and stir fry red curry paste until fragrant. Add coconut milk and bring to a boil. Add the next 5 ingredients, and let simmer for 5 minutes on medium heat. Add prawns and cook for another minute. Remove from heat and serve. Serves four.

Wine Recommendations:

Chardonnay
Gewürtztraminer

Red Pork Curry

1	tablespoon vegetable oil
3	tablespoons red curry paste
3	cups coconut milk
1	cup lean pork, thinly sliced
½	cup shredded young bamboo shoots
3	kaffir lime leaves
10	basil leaves
3	tablespoons fish sauce
3	red chili peppers, chopped (optional)

Heat oil and stir fry red curry paste until fragrant. Add coconut milk and bring to a boil. Add pork and cook for 3 minutes, or until pork is done. Add remaining ingredients and cook for about 8 more minutes. Serves four.

Wine Recommendations:

Dry Reisling
Zinfandel

Roast Duck Curry

1	tablespoon vegetable oil
3	cups coconut milk
3	tablespoons red curry paste
2	cups roast duck, deboned and cut into 1-inch strips
1	cup eggplant, sliced thinly
1	large tomato, sliced
1	cup pineapple, chopped
2	kaffir lime leaves, cut in half
3	tablespoons fish sauce

Heat oil and stir fry red curry paste until fragrant. Add coconut milk and bring to a boil. Add remaining ingredients and cook for 5 minutes. Serves four.

Wine Recommendations:

Dry Reisling
Zinfandel

82

Steamed Pork, Fish & Chicken Curry

banana or pandan leaves
2   tablespoons red curry paste
3   cups coconut milk
1   cup pork, thinly sliced
1   cup chicken, thinly sliced
1   cup fish fillet, thinly sliced
2   eggs
1   red chili, thinly sliced
10 basil leaves
3   kaffir lime leaves, thinly sliced
3   tablespoons fish sauce
    cilantro for garnishing

Line the steamer with pandan or banana leaves. Mix the ingredients together and pour the mixture into the steamer. Steam for 15 minutes. Remove steamer, top with chopped cilantro leaves and serve. Serves four.

Wine Recommendations:

Gewürtztraminer
Pinot Noir

83

Thai Crab Curry

2-3 pounds whole cooked crabs
1 tablespoon vegetable oil
3 tablespoons yellow curry paste
1 cup coconut milk
3 tablespoons fish sauce
1 tablespoon brown sugar or honey
2 red chilies, julienned
1 onion, chopped
green onions and cilantro for garnish

Cut crabs into serving pieces. Leave shells on but crack them. In a wok, brown the garlic in oil and stir fry the yellow curry paste until fragrant. Add crabs, followed by remaining ingredients. Stir fry for 5 minutes. Garnish with green onions and cilantro. Serve immediately. Serves four.

Wine Recommendations:

Dry Reisling
Pinot Noir

Thai Crab Curry **85**

Phuket Seafood

SEAFOOD

Basil Scallops
Clams with Basil
Garlic Calamari
Green Curry Prawns and Calamari
Lobster with Hot Sauce
Prawns with String Beans
Sizzling Fish
Sizzling Salmon
Spicy Basil Prawns
Spicy Mussels
Steamed Clams with Fresh Ginger
Steamed Garlic Prawns
Steamed Seafood Combination

Basil Scallops

3	tablespoons olive oil
1	tablespoon chopped garlic
$\frac{1}{2}$	cup chopped onion
1	cup scallops
10	basil sprigs
$\frac{1}{2}$	cup baby corn
3	tablespoons fish sauce
2	red chili, seeds removed

Brown the garlic in oil. Add onions and scallops, cooking for 2 minutes. Add remaining ingredients and stir fry the mixture for 3 minutes until done. Serves four.

Wine Recommendations:

Pinot Gris
Sauvignon Blanc

Clams with Basil

2	tablespoons olive oil
2	tablespoons garlic, crushed
2	green onions, cut in half
4	green chilies, cut lengthwise
4	red chilies, cut lengthwise
20	basil leaves
2	pounds fresh clams, steamed, cleaned, shelled and drained
4	tablespoons fish sauce
3	tablespoons lime juice
	cilantro and green onions for garnish

Brown the garlic in oil, then add all ingredients. Stir fry for 4-5 minutes over high heat. Pour into large platter and garnish with cilantro and green onions. Serves four.

Wine Recommendations:

Merlot
Semillon

Garlic Calamari

2	tablespoons vegetable oil
2	cups calamari, cut diagonally with a criss-cross pattern
5	tablespoons garlic, chopped
1	small onion, chopped
1	small red bell pepper, sliced
½	cup carrots, chopped
1	tablespoon oyster sauce
2	tablespoons fish sauce
	cilantro and green onions for garnish

Brown the garlic in oil. Add onions and calamari and stir fry for 2 minutes. Add remaining ingredients and cook for 5 minutes. Garnish with finely sliced green onions and cilantro. Serves four.

Wine Recommendations:

Fruity Merlot

Green Curry Prawns and Calamari

2	tablespoons olive oil
1	tablespoon garlic, chopped
3	tablespoons green curry
1	small onion, chopped
6	prawns, shelled and deveined
1	cup calamari, sliced diagonally
2	tablespoons fish sauce
2	tablespoons oyster sauce
½	cup green and red sliced peppers

Brown the garlic. Add curry and onions. Cook for 1-2 minutes.
Add remaining ingredients and cook for 5 minutes. Serves four.

Wine Recommendations:

Chardonnay

Lobster with Hot Sauce

1½ pound lobster, live

Sauce:
2   tablespoons fish sauce
2   tablespoons soy sauce
2   red chilies, thinly sliced
2   green chilies, thinly sliced
4   wedges of lime for garnish

Steam lobster for 15 minutes. Place on a platter. Garnish with fresh vegetables. Combine sauce ingredients and serve for dipping. *See illustration on page 92.* Serves four.

Wine Recommendations:

**Chardonnay
Pinot Gris**

Lobster with Hot Sauce　　**93**

Prawns with String Beans

2	tablespoons vegetable oil
1	tablespoon garlic, chopped
1	small onion, chopped
2	cups string beans, cut into 2-inch lengths
8	prawns, shelled and deveined
2	tablespoons fish sauce
2	tablespoons oyster sauce
2	red chilis, seeded and sliced lengthwise
1	small carrot, sliced thinly
	green onions and cilantro for garnish

Brown the garlic in oil. Add onions and beans. Cook for 3 minutes. Add remaining ingredients and stir fry till prawns are cooked. Garnish with cilantro and green onions. Serves four.

Wine Recommendations:

Semillon

Sizzling Fish

1	pound Pomfret or any similar fish, deep-fried
1	tablespoon garlic, chopped
1	small onion, chopped
5	basil sprigs
1	cup tamarind sweet and sour sauce
1	tablespoon fish sauce
1	tablespoon oyster sauce
$\frac{1}{2}$	cup red and green peppers, sliced
2	tablespoons sliced pineapples

Place fried fish on a hot plate and keep over low heat until sauce is ready. In a saucepan, brown garlic and onions. Add remaining ingredients and mix for 3 minutes. Serve immediately, pouring the sauce over the fish to produce the sizzling effect. Serves four.

Note: Tamarind sauce may be substituted with ½ cup lime juice and ½ brown sugar boiled for 3 minutes.

Wine Recommendations:

Fruity Cabernet
Merlot

Sizzling Salmon

1	large salmon steak, deep-fried
1	tablespoon garlic, chopped
1	small onion, chopped
5	basil sprigs
1	cup tamarind sweet and sour sauce
1	tablespoon fish sauce
1	tablespoon oyster sauce
½	cup red and green peppers, sliced
2	tablespoons pineapples, sliced

Place fried salmon on a hot plate and keep over low heat until sauce is ready. In a saucepan, brown garlic and onions. Add remaining ingredients and mix for 3 minutes. Serve immediately, pouring the sauce over the fish to produce the sizzling effect. Serves four.

Wine Recommendations:

Fruity Cabernet
Merlot

Spicy Basil Prawns

3   tablespoons vegetable oil
1   tablespoon garlic, chopped
1   small onion, chopped
8   prawns, shelled and deveined
10 basil leaves
2   tablespoons fish sauce
4   red spur chilies, cut in half
1   teaspoon shrimp paste

Brown the garlic in oil on medium heat. Add remaining ingredients and stir fry until done. Serves four.

Wine Recommendations:

Fruity Merlot
Semillon

Spicy Mussels

2	tablespoons vegetable oil
4	tablespoons garlic, finely chopped
1	medium onion, finely chopped
12	mussels, each on a half-shell
½	cup water or broth
1	tablespoon yellow bean sauce
2	tablespoons oyster sauce
1	tablespoon dark soy sauce
5	red chili peppers, cut in half
2	green onions, cut into 1-inch lengths
2	tablespoons cilantro

Brown the garlic in oil. Add onions and mussels. Stir fry for 5 minutes. Add remaining ingredients and cook for another 5 minutes. Serve hot. Serves four.

Wine Recommendations:

Dry Reisling
Merlot

Steamed Clams with Fresh Ginger

2   tablespoons vegetable oil
2   tablespoons garlic, chopped
1   small onion, thinly sliced
2   pounds fresh clams, rinsed
3   green onions, cut into 2-inch lengths
2   tablespoons fresh ginger, thinly sliced
2   tablespoons yellow bean sauce
1   tablespoon oyster sauce
1-2 red chili peppers, seeded and cut into thin strips
    cilantro for garnish

Brown the garlic in oil and add onions. Combine remaining ingredients and steam for 15 minutes or until clams open. Garnish with cilantro. Serves four.

Wine Recommendations:

Fumé Blanc
Semillon

Steamed Garlic Prawns

12	prawns, shelled and deveined
3	tablespoons vegetable oil
5	tablespoons garlic, chopped
1	green onion, cut in half
2	tablespoons oyster sauce
1	teaspoon white pepper

Wash and drain prawns. Line steamer with a plate or banana or pandan leaves and steam the prawns for 8-10 minutes. Next, brown garlic and add remaining ingredients. Serve prawns on platter. Serves four.

Wine Recommendations:

Pinot Gris
Sauvignon Blanc

Steamed Seafood Combination

6	prawns, shelled and deveined
1	cup scallops
4	mussels, on half-shells
2	slices of fish
$\frac{1}{2}$	cup squid, sliced
4	tablespoons green curry paste
1	cup coconut milk
4	tablespoons fish sauce
1	stalk lemon grass, cut diagonally in 1-inch lengths
1	cup red and green peppers, sliced
10	basil tips
	cilantro and green onions for garnish

In a steamer, mix everything together and steam for 15 minutes. Garnish with cilantro and green onions. Serves four.

Wine Recommendations:

Chardonnay
Pinot Gris

101

Thai Orchids

MEATS AND VEGETABLES

Beef with Oyster Sauce
Beef with String Beans and Fresh Ginger
Cashew Chicken
Chicken with Basil
Chicken with Black Mushrooms
Chicken with Fresh Ginger
Chicken Jungle King
Chili Pork with String Beans
Eggplant with Chicken
Honey Duckling
Ostrich Jungle King
Roast Duck with Chili
Spicy Chicken with Basil
Sweet and Sour Chicken
Thai Barbecue Chicken
Thai Eggplant with Chicken

Beef with Oyster Sauce

2	tablespoons vegetable oil
2	tablespoons garlic, chopped
1	cup fresh mushrooms, soaked in water and cut in half
$\frac{1}{2}$	cup carrots, julienne cut
$\frac{1}{2}$	cup baby corn
$\frac{1}{2}$	cup bok choy, chopped
2	cups flank steak, thinly sliced
3	tablespoons oyster sauce

Brown the garlic in oil and add beef. Cook for 3 minutes. Add the remaining ingredients and cook for 5 minutes, and then serve. Serves four.

Wine Recommendations:

Merlot
Zinfandel

Beef with Oyster Sauce

105

Beef with String Beans and Fresh Ginger

2	tablespoons vegetable oil
2	tablespoons garlic, chopped
1	small onion, chopped
2	cups beef, thinly sliced
2	cups string beans, julienne cut and steamed
2	tablespoons ginger, thinly sliced
2	red chili peppers, cut in half (optional)
2	tablespoons fish sauce
2	tablespoons oyster sauce

Brown the garlic and onion in oil, adding the beef and string beans. Cook for 5 minutes. Add remaining ingredients and cook until beef is done. Serve immediately. Serves four.

Wine Recommendations:

Cabernet Sauvignon
Syrah

Cashew Chicken

2	cups chicken breast, thinly sliced
2	tablespoons cornstarch
2	tablespoons soy sauce
$\frac{1}{2}$	cup sweet wine (optional)
$\frac{1}{4}$	cup vegetable oil
2	cloves garlic, crushed
1	small onion, chopped
2	green onions, cut into 2-inch lengths
2	tablespoons oyster sauce
5	whole dried red chili peppers
4	tablespoons roasted cashew nuts, unsalted
4	tablespoons water chestnuts, chopped

Marinate chicken in soy sauce, wine, and cornstarch for 5 minutes. Brown the garlic in oil and add onion and chicken. Cook for 5-8 minutes, or until chicken is done. Add remaining ingredients, except for cashew nuts, and cook for 3 minutes. Remove from heat and add cashew nuts. Serve immediately. Serves four.

Wine Recommendations:

Chardonnay
Pinot Noir

107

Chicken with Basil

3 tablespoons vegetable oil
2 tablespoons garlic, chopped
2 cups chicken breast, thinly sliced
1 small onion, chopped
3 kaffir lime leaves, cut in thin strips
1 cup mushrooms, cut in half
3 tablespoons oyster sauce
2 tablespoons fish sauce
6 red chili peppers, cut in half or 1 small red bell pepper, chopped
1 cup basil leaves

Brown the garlic in oil, then add chicken and onions and cook for 5 minutes, or until chicken is done. Add remaining ingredients and stir fry for another 3-5 minutes. Serve immediately. Serves four.

Wine Recommendations:

Rhōne Reds
Zinfandel

Chicken with Black Mushrooms

2 tablespoons vegetable oil
1 tablespoon garlic, chopped
1 pound boneless chicken breast, thinly sliced
10 large dried Chinese black mushrooms, soaked and with stems removed
1 onion, chopped
1 tablespoon ginger, shredded
3 tablespoons fish sauce
1 teaspoon sugar

Brown the garlic in oil, then add chicken and cook for 5 minutes or until done. Add remaining ingredients and stir fry for another 2 minutes. Serve immediately. Serves four.

Wine Recommendations:

Cabernet
Zinfandel

Chicken with Fresh Ginger

2   tablespoons vegetable oil
2   tablespoons garlic
1   onion, chopped
½   cup young ginger, thinly sliced into 1-inch lengths
1   cup thinly sliced chicken breast
8   dried black mushrooms, soaked and with stems removed
1   tomato, sliced
3   green onions
2   red chilies, cut in half (optional)
1   teaspoon sugar
2   tablespoons fish sauce

Brown the garlic in oil, then add onion, ginger and chicken and stir fry for 5 minutes or until chicken is done. Add remaining ingredients and stir fry for 3-5 minutes. Serve immediately. Serves four.

Wine Recommendations:

**Light Fruity Cabernet
Zinfandel**

Chicken Jungle King

2	tablespoons vegetable oil
2	tablespoons garlic, chopped
3	tablespoons red curry paste
1	small onion, chopped
2	cups chicken breast, thinly sliced
6	small red chili peppers, cut in half
1	stalk fresh lemon grass, thinly sliced
2	kaffir lime leaves, cut in half
$\frac{1}{4}$	cup baby corn, halved
$\frac{1}{2}$	cup mushrooms
$\frac{1}{2}$	cup coconut milk
2	tablespoons fish sauce
2	tablespoon oyster sauce
10-15	basil leaves

Brown the garlic in oil and add red curry paste, followed by onions and the chicken. Cook for 5 minutes or until chicken is done. Add remaining ingredients and cook for another 3 minutes. Serve immediately. Serves four.

Wine Recommendations:

**Gewürtztraminer
San Giovese**

Chili Pork with String Beans

2   tablespoons vegetable oil
1   tablespoon garlic, chopped
4   tablespoons red chili paste
2   cups pork, thinly sliced
4   cups string beans, cut into 1-inch lengths
1   teaspoon kaffir lime leaves, minced
4   red chilies, sliced lengthwise
1   tablespoon sugar
2   tablespoons fish sauce

Brown the garlic in oil, then add pork and chili paste and cook until pork is done. Add string beans and stir fry for 5 minutes. Add remaining ingredients and stir fry for another 2 minutes. Serve immediately. Serves four.

Wine Recommendations:

Semillon
Zinfandel

Eggplant with Chicken

3	tablespoons vegetable oil
1	tablespoon garlic, chopped
1	cup chicken breast, thinly sliced
3	cups purple eggplant, sliced crosswise to about ¼-inch thickness
4	red chili peppers, cut lengthwise
10	sweet basil leaves
3	tablespoons yellow bean sauce
4	tablespoons oyster sauce
1	cup chicken stock

Brown the garlic in oil and add chicken and eggplant. Cook for 5 minutes or until chicken is done. Add remaining ingredients and stir fry for another 3 minutes. Serve immediately. Serves four.

Wine Recommendations:

Gewürtztraminer
Syrah

Honey Duckling

1	duck, about 3 pounds
2	tablespoons garlic, chopped
2	tablespoons five spice powder
1	tablespoon palm sugar
1	tablespoon honey
1	tablespoon lime juice
2	tablespoons garlic salt
1	tablespoon fresh ginger, chopped
2	tablespoons soy sauce
	green onions and cilantro for garnish

Rinse duck and pat dry. Combine remaining ingredients in a food processor or blender and blend until smooth. Rub mixture all over and inside the duck. Preheat oven to 375°F and bake duck for 1 hour or until done. Serve with Hot Chili Sweet Sauce (*refer to page 144*) or dark soy sauce topped with finely chopped green onions and cilantro.

Wine Recommendations:

Champagne
Merlot

114

Honey Duckling **115**

Ostrich Jungle King

2	tablespoons vegetable oil
2	tablespoons garlic, chopped
3	tablespoons red curry
1	cup ostrich meat, sliced thinly
$\frac{1}{2}$	cup coconut milk
2	tablespoons fish sauce
2	tablespoons oyster sauce
10	basil leaves
1	cup green and red peppers, sliced
$\frac{1}{2}$	cup baby corn
$\frac{1}{2}$	cup mushrooms, sliced

Brown the garlic in oil and add red curry, followed by ostrich meat. Cook for 6-8 minutes. Stir in remaining ingredients and cook for another 3-5 minutes. Serve immediately. Serves four.

Wine Recommendations:

Bordeaux
Cabernet Sauvignon
Rhōne Reds
Rioja

Roast Duck with Chili

1	roast duck, cut into serving pieces
2	tablespoons vegetable oil
2	tablespoons garlic, chopped
1	small onion, chopped
10	red chili peppers, soaked, drained, and seeded
2	tablespoons fish sauce
2	tablespoons soy sauce
1	tablespoon brown sugar or honey
	cilantro and green onions for garnish

Brown the garlic in oil and add onion and duck, followed by the remaining ingredients. Cook for 6-8 minutes. Garnish with green onions and cilantro. Serve immediately. Serves four.

Wine Recommendations:

Syrah
Zinfandel

Spicy Chicken with Basil

2 tablespoons vegetable oil
2 tablespoons garlic, chopped
1 cup chicken, chopped
3 kaffir lime leaves, cut in thin strips
½ cup mushrooms (preferably straw mushrooms)
¼ cup bamboo shoots, sliced
3 tablespoons oyster sauce
3 red chili peppers, seeded and chopped (optional)
12 basil leaves

Brown the garlic in oil. Add chicken and cook for 3 minutes. Add remaining ingredients, except the basil. Cook for 5 minutes. Add basil and serve. Serves four.

Wine Recommendations:

Lemberger
Rhōne Reds

Spicy Chicken with Basil **119**

Sweet and Sour Chicken

2	tablespoons vegetable oil
1	tablespoon garlic, chopped
2	cups chicken, julienne cut
$\frac{1}{2}$	cup cucumber or zucchini, cubed
$\frac{1}{2}$	cup green and red bell peppers, cubed
$\frac{1}{2}$	cup onions, cubed
$\frac{1}{2}$	cup pineapple chunks
$\frac{1}{2}$	cup tomatoes, diced
2	tablespoons fish sauce
2	tablespoons catsup
$\frac{1}{2}$	cup soup stock or water
1	teaspoon cornstarch mixed with 2 tablespoons water

Brown the garlic in oil, then add chicken and cook it till done. Add rest of the ingredients, except for the cornstarch mixture, and stir fry for 3-4 minutes or until done. Add the cornstarch to thicken the mixture and let cook for another minute before removing the pan from the heat. Serve immediately. Serves four.

Wine Recommendations:

Dolcetto
Fume Rosé
Zinfandel

120

Sweet and Sour Chicken

Thai Baked Chicken

2	whole young chickens, quartered
4	stalks fresh lemon grass, thinly sliced
2	tablespoons fresh ginger, chopped
2	tablespoons garlic, finely chopped
½	cup cilantro
3	tablespoons brown sugar
1	cup coconut milk
2	tablespoons fish sauce
2	tablespoons soy sauce
2	tablespoons vegetable oil
2	tablespoons yellow curry

Place chickens in a large bowl. In a food processor or blender, combine all the remaining ingredients and blend until smooth. Pour the sauce over the chickens and marinate for 4 hours or overnight in the refrigerator. Preheat oven to 350°F. Place chickens on a rack in an open pan with the split side down. Bake for about an hour or until done. Cut the quarters into smaller pieces and arrange on a serving platter. Garnish with cilantro and serve with Hot Chili Sweet Sauce (*refer to page 144*). Serves four.

Wine Recommendations:

Chardonnay
Zinfandel

Thai Eggplant with Chicken

8	Thai eggplants, quartered
1	cup chicken breast, thinly sliced
5	tablespoons vegetable oil
2	tablespoons crushed garlic
5	red chilies, seeded and chopped
$\frac{1}{2}$	cup chicken stock
4	tablespoons fish sauce
1	tablespoon oyster sauce
8	basil sprigs

Brown the garlic in oil. Add chicken and cook until done. Add all remaining ingredients except the last and cook for 5 minutes. Add basil and serve immediately. Serves four.

124 *Fresh Garden Rolls with Peanut Sauce*

VEGETARIAN

Asparagus with Black Mushrooms
Broccoli in Oyster Sauce
Broccoli with Rice Noodles
Mixed Mushrooms with Baby Corn
Mixed Vegetables with Tofu
Spicy Asparagus with Tofu
Spinach in Peanut Sauce
Stir Fried Ong Choi with Yellow Bean Sauce
Stir Fried Mixed Vegetables
String Beans with Fresh Ginger
Vegetarian Jungle King

Asparagus with Black Mushrooms

2   tablespoons vegetable oil
1   tablespoon garlic, chopped
1   pound fresh asparagus, julienne cut
10 black mushrooms, soaked, drained and without stems
4   tablespoons oyster sauce
6   red chili peppers, cut in half or 1 small red bell pepper, chopped (optional)

Brown the garlic in oil and add remaining ingredients. Stir fry for 3-5 minutes. Serve immediately. Serves four.

Wine Recommendations:

Fruity Wine

126

Broccoli in Oyster Sauce

5   tablespoons vegetable oil
1   tablespoon garlic, chopped
4   cups broccoli crowns, cut lengthwise
6   tablespoons oyster sauce

Brown the garlic in oil, then add broccoli and stir fry for 3-4 minutes. Add oyster sauce and stir fry for another minute. Serve immediately. Serves four.

Wine Recommendations:

Chardonnay

Broccoli with Rice Noodles

4   tablespoons vegetable oil
2   tablespoons garlic, chopped
1   pound large rice noodles, soaked in water
4   cups broccoli crowns, sliced and blanched
1   egg
2   tablespoons dark soy sauce
2   tablespoons oyster sauce
1   teaspoon sugar

Brown the garlic in oil. Add noodles, and stir fry for 2 minutes. Combine broccoli and remaining ingredients. Stir fry for another 3-4 minutes. Serve immediately. Serves four.

Wine Recommendations:

Chardonnay

Mixed Mushrooms with Baby Corn

4   tablespoons vegetable oil
2   tablespoons garlic, chopped
1   small onion, chopped
1   cup Chinese mushrooms, cut in half
1   cup straw mushrooms, cut in half
1   cup crimini mushrooms
10   baby corn, sliced in half lengthwise
2   tablespoons fish sauce
1   tablespoon soy sauce
1   tablespoon oyster sauce
1   teaspoon tapioca flour dissolved in 3 tablespoons water
     chili and cilantro for garnish

Brown the garlic in oil. Add onions and mushrooms. Stir fry for 2 minutes. Add remaining 4 ingredients and mix for 2 minutes. Add tapioca flour mixture and stir fry for one minute. Garnish with chili and cilantro. Serve immediately. Serves four.

Wine Recommendations:

Chardonnay

Mixed Vegetables with Tofu

4   tablespoons vegetable oil
1   tablespoon garlic, chopped
3   tablespoons oyster sauce
1   small onion, chopped
5   cups bean sprouts
2   tablespoons green onion, cut into 1-inch lengths
3   tablespoons cilantro leaves
1   cup sliced tofu, fresh or fried

Brown the garlic in oil and then add remaining ingredients and stir fry for 3 minutes. Serve immediately. Serves four.

Wine Recommendations:

Chardonnay

Mixed Vegetables with Tofu　　**131**

Spicy Asparagus with Tofu

5   tablespoons vegetable oil
2   tablespoons red curry paste
2   tablespoons garlic, chopped
4   cups asparagus, julienne cut
2   tablespoons oyster sauce
1   tablespoon soy sauce
1   teaspoon sugar

Brown the garlic in oil, then add red curry paste and fry for 1 minute. Add asparagus and stir fry for 2 minutes. Add remaining ingredients and cook for 2-3 minutes. Serve immediately. Serves four.

Wine Recommendations:

Sauvignon Blanc

Spinach in Peanut Sauce

4	tablespoons vegetable oil
1	tablespoon garlic, chopped
6	cups spinach, cut in half
5	tablespoons peanut sauce

Brown the garlic in oil, then add spinach and stir fry for 2-3 minutes. Do not overcook. Top with Peanut Sauce (*refer to page 147*). Serves four.

Wine Recommendations:

Chardonnay

Stir Fried Ong Choi with Yellow Bean Sauce

4   **tablespoons vegetable oil**
2   **tablespoons garlic, finely chopped**
4   **cups ong choi or watercress, cut into 2-inch lengths**
1   **tablespoon yellow bean sauce**
2   **tablespoons oyster sauce**
4   **red chili peppers, cut in half (optional)**

Brown the garlic in oil and add remaining ingredients. Cook for 3-5 minutes. Serves four.

Note: Broccoli, cabbage, cauliflower, spinach, or watercress can be substituted for ong choi.

Wine Recommendations:

Sauvignon Blanc

Stir Fried Mixed Vegetables

2	tablespoons vegetable oil
2	tablespoons garlic, chopped
1	small onion, chopped
1	cup chicken stock
½	cup broccoli crowns, cut into bite-sized pieces
½	cup cauliflower, cut into bite-sized pieces
½	cup snow peas
½	cup small mushrooms or crimini
½	cup carrots, sliced
5	tablespoons oyster sauce
1	tablespoon soy sauce

Brown the garlic in oil, then add onion and chicken stock. Add remaining ingredients and stir fry for 4-6 minutes. Vegetables should only be half-cooked when served. Serves four.

Wine Recommendations:

Dry/ Fruity Reisling

String Beans with Fresh Ginger

2	tablespoons vegetable oil
1	tablespoon garlic, chopped
3	cups fresh string beans, cut into 2-inch lengths
2	tablespoons ginger, thinly sliced
4	red chili peppers, cut in half
½	cup coconut milk
½	cup fried tofu, sliced (optional)

Brown the garlic in oil and add remaining ingredients. Stir fry for 5 minutes. Serve immediately. Serves four.

Wine Recommendations:

Sauvignon Blanc

Vegetarian Jungle King

2	tablespoons vegetable oil
1	tablespoon garlic, chopped
$\frac{1}{2}$	cup baby corn
$\frac{1}{2}$	cup mushrooms
$\frac{1}{2}$	cup red and green bell peppers, chopped
4	small red chili peppers, cut in half
2	tablespoons oyster sauce
2	tablespoons fish sauce
$\frac{1}{2}$	cup coconut milk
12	sweet basil leaves
1	cup cabbage, chopped

Brown the garlic in oil and add remaining ingredients. Stir fry for 5-6 minutes. Serve immediately. Serves four.

Wine Recommendations:

Sauvignon Blanc

138   *Assorted Sauces*

SAUCES, DIPS, & CURRY PASTES

Black Chili Paste
Chili in Vinegar
Cucumber Sauce
Fish Sauce with Chili
Garlic Pickle
Ginger Pickle
Green Curry Paste
Green Mango Dip
Hot Chili Sweet Sauce
Mussaman Curry Paste
Panang Curry Paste
Peanut Sauce for Satay
Red Curry Paste
Spicy Mango Pickle
Spring Roll Sauce
Yellow Curry Paste
Young Tamarind Paste

Black Chili Paste

1	cup vegetable oil, for deep-frying
6	dried green jalapeno peppers
1	cup shallots, chopped
1	cup garlic, chopped
8	ounces dried shrimp/prawns
2	tablespoons shrimp paste
4	tablespoons fish sauce
¼	cup sugar

Heat the oil and deep-fry dried peppers, shallots and garlic until dark brown. Combine all the ingredients in a blender, and process until smooth mixture forms. Pour entire mixture into a medium skillet and fry on medium heat for 5 minutes. Remove, cool, and place in jar with a tight lid. It will keep indefinitely.

Chili in Vinegar

4 green jalapeño peppers, sliced in rounds
2 red jalapeño peppers, sliced in rounds
½ cup vinegar
1 teaspoon salt

Combine peppers, vinegar, and salt. Use as a sauce or dip for noodles or to improve or change the flavor of other dishes.

Cucumber Sauce

1	cucumber, thinly sliced
6	tablespoons sugar
1	cup boiling water
½	cup vinegar
1	teaspoon salt
1	red chili, chopped
2	shallots, finely sliced
	cilantro

Dissolve sugar in boiling water and stir in vinegar and salt. Pour over cucumber slices and sprinkle chili and shallots over the mixture. Garnish with cilantro.

Fish Sauce with Chili

¼	cup fish sauce
5	tablespoons lemon or lime juice
2	garlic cloves, minced
4	green chili peppers, chopped
4	red chili peppers, chopped

Combine all ingredients and use as a dipping sauce. This sauce can be used in curries or stir-fried dishes.

Garlic Pickle

2   cups water
2   cups garlic cloves, peeled, boiled and drained
2   cups vinegar
2   cups sugar
2   tablespoons salt

Combine all ingredients and bring to a boil for 3 minutes. When cooled, transfer to a glass jar and store in refrigerator for one week before using.

Ginger Pickle

2   cups vinegar
2   cups water
¼   cup salt
2   cups sugar
2   cups fresh ginger, thinly sliced

Combine all ingredients and bring to a boil for 10 minutes. Place in a jar and store in refrigerator for a week before using.

Green Curry Paste

10	green jalapeno peppers
5	green chili peppers
½	cup sliced cilantro/coriander root or stems
8	garlic cloves
¼	cup chopped shallots or purple onions
¼	cup chopped lemon grass
5	thin slices fresh galanga
1	teaspoon cumin
1	teaspoon shrimp paste

Combine all ingredients in a blender and process until smooth. Keep in an airtight container and refrigerate. Paste wiill keep for 1 year.

Green Mango Dip

2	cups green mango, finely shredded
1	tablespoon garlic, finely chopped
2	tablespoons shrimp paste
¼	cup fish sauce
2	tablespoons lime juice
2	tablespoons sugar

Place shredded mango, garlic, and shrimp paste in a mortar and gently mash with pestle so the mango is bruised but is in shreds. Add remaining ingredients and continue to pound. Spoon over a bed of lettuce and use as a dip for grilled meats or fresh vegetables.

Hot Chili Sweet Sauce

1   cup water
1   cup brown sugar
½   cup vinegar
½   cup dried red chili, crushed
1   tablespoon salt
1   tablespoon garlic, crushed

Boil water in a saucepan then lower heat and add all ingredients.
Bring to a boil once more for 2 minutes. Let cool before using.
Can be kept in refrigerator for five months.

Mussamun Curry Paste

5 tablespoons vegetable oil
4 dried jalapeño peppers
½ cup onions, chopped
½ cup garlic cloves, chopped
1 tablespoon lemon grass, chopped
2 thin slices galanga
2 shallots
¼ teaspoon kaffir lime skin
2 tablespoons dried cilantro
1 tablespoon cumin
1 teaspoon cinnamon powder
1 tablespoon star anise powder

Brown the garlic in oil and add peppers and onions. Combine all ingredients in a blender. Blend until a paste is formed. Store in airtight container. Can be kept in refrigerator for up to 1 year.

Panang Curry Paste

4	ounces dried green jalapeño peppers
¼	cup coriander seed
½	cup chopped onions or shallots
½	cup chopped garlic
2	tablespoons galanga, chopped
¼	cup lemon grass, chopped
2	tablespoons shrimp paste
1	teaspoon salt

Blend all ingredients in a processor until a paste is formed. Store in a jar with a tight lid for future use. Can be kept in refrigerator for one year.

Peanut Sauce for Satay

1	tablespoon red curry paste
1	tablespoon sugar
3	tablespoons peanut butter, creamy or chunky
2	cups coconut milk
1	teaspoon tamarind juice or lime juice
1	teaspoon salt

Bring coconut milk to a boil. Add red curry paste and stir. Add remaining ingredients and cook until smooth.

Red Curry Paste

$\frac{1}{2}$	cup onions, chopped
8	garlic cloves
10	dried red jalapeño chilies
4	fresh galanga, thin slices
2	tablespoons lemon grass, chopped
1	tablespoon cilantro, chopped
$\frac{1}{2}$	teaspoon shrimp paste
1	teaspoon salt
3	tablespoons oil

Combine all ingredients except the oil in a blender and process until smooth. In a small skillet on medium high heat, fry curry paste for 5 minutes until fragrant. Remove and store in a jar for future use. Can be kept in refrigerator for 1 year.

Spicy Mango Pickle

4	cups water
1	cup salt
1	cup sugar
2	red chilies, thinly sliced
6	cups green mangoes, peeled and sliced

Combine first 4 ingredients in a saucepan. Bring to a boil, then set aside and allow to cool. Pour the pickling solution over mangoes and store. Set aside for at least 1 week before eating. Can be kept in refrigerator for 1 year.

Spring Roll Sauce

½	cup sugar
½	cup vinegar
½	cup water
2	tablespoons fish sauce
1	teaspoon ground red chili
½	cup carrots, shredded

In a small saucepan, bring sugar and water to a boil until sugar is dissolved. Add vinegar, fish sauce, chili and carrots and bring mixture to a boil once more. Pour sauce into a serving bowl.

Yellow Curry Paste

10   dried chilies, chopped
1   onion, chopped
2   tablespoons garlic, chopped
2   tablespoons cilantro, chopped
2   tablespoons fresh lemongrass, chopped
2   tablespoons cumin
1   tablespoon ground turmeric
1   teaspoon salt

Blend all ingredients in a processor until a paste is formed. Store in a jar with a tight seal for future use. Can be kept in refrigerator for 1 year.

Young Tamarind Paste

¼   cup dried shrimp
1   cup young tamarind, peeled and chopped
3   tablespoons garlic, chopped
2   tablespoons shrimp paste
5   tablespoons fish sauce
2   tablespoons lime juice
3   tablespoons sugar
3   tablespoons vegetable oil

In a mortar, pound the dried shrimp, young tamarind, garlic, and shrimp paste. Add the fish sauce, lime juice, and sugar. In a saucepan, heat oil and stir fry the mixture until it forms a paste. Use at once. Can be kept in refrigerator for 1 year.

Carved Fresh Fruits

DESSERTS

Banana Fritters
Black Rice Pudding
Coconut Balls
Crispy Sweet Bananas
Golden Silk Threads
Pumpkin Custard
Rice Balls in Coconut Milk
Sweet Rice with Fresh Mango
Sweet Rice Pudding
Sweet Taro Pudding
Tapioca Delight
Thai Custard
Water Chestnut Cooler

Black Rice Pudding

Banana Fritters

1	egg
2	tablespoons sugar
1	cup flour
$\frac{1}{4}$	cup cornstarch
$\frac{1}{2}$	teaspoon salt
1	teaspoon baking powder
$\frac{1}{2}$	cup milk or coconut milk
2	cups vegetable oil
6	ripe cooking bananas
2	tablespoons honey

Mix first 6 ingredients together in a mixing bowl. Peel bananas and cut into pieces about 2 inches in length. Dip into batter and deep fry for 3-7 minutes or until golden brown. Drain and sweeten with honey.

Black Rice Pudding

2	cups black rice, washed, soaked overnight and drained
4	cups water
3	cups coconut milk
1	cup white sugar
a pinch of salt	

In a medium-sized uncovered pot, bring rice and water to a boil over high heat for 3 minutes, stirring occasionally. Reduce heat to low. Cover pot and let simmer for 1 hour or until rice is soft. Let rice cool. In a saucepan, cook coconut milk, sugar, and salt over low heat for 20 minutes. To serve, put 2 tablespoons of pudding on a dish and top with 2 tablespoons of coconut mixture.

Coconut Balls

1¼ cups water
1½ cups sugar
1   teaspoon jasmine extract
2   drops food coloring (optional)
2½ cups shredded coconut
a pinch of salt

In a saucepan, heat water, sugar, and salt on medium heat and stir until mixture is syrupy. Add jasmine and food coloring, and mix in the flaked coconut to absorb the liquid. In 1 tablespoon portions, place candy about 2 inches apart on a plate lined with waxed paper and allow to cool before serving.

Crispy Sweet Bananas

8   green bananas, sliced long and thin
5   cups vegetable oil

Syrup:
2   cup sugar
2   cup water
2   drops jasmine flavoring
a pinch of salt

Deep-fry bananas until golden brown and crispy. Set aside to cool. In a separate saucepan, combine all ingredients for the syrup and boil for 3 minutes. Dip bananas into syrup and quickly remove. Serve either hot or cold.

Golden Silk Threads

12 egg yolks
1   teaspoon egg white
3   cups sugar
1   cup water
2   drops jasmine flavoring
5   fine-point paper cones

Roll bond paper into cones and then cut off the pointed tips. Beat the egg yolks and egg white together, then put into a container. Strain egg mixture through a fine sieve. In a saucepan, heat sugar, water and jasmine flavoring. Pour about 4 cups of the egg yolk mixture into a fine-point paper cone, moving very rapidly around the pan of syrup until you get very fine but unbroken lines of the yolk in the boiling syrup. The egg strings cook very quickly so remove them almost at once with chopsticks or a slotted spoon. Add a little boiling water to the syrup each time before repeating the process.

Pumpkin Custard

6   eggs
1   cup coconut cream
1   cup palm or brown sugar
1   whole small pumpkin

Beat eggs with coconut cream and sugar until the mixture is frothy. Remove the top of the pumpkin and carefully scoop out the seeds and any fibers. Pour in the coconut cream mixture; cover with the pumpkin top and place in a steamer. Cover the steamer and place over boiling water. Cook for about 20 minutes or until the mixture has set. Allow to cool and cut in thick slices to serve.

Rice Balls in Coconut Milk

3   cups glutinous rice flour
4   cups coconut cream
2   cups sugar
a pinch of salt

Mix rice flour with enough water to make a stiff paste. Knead well and then form into marble-sized balls. Boil a large pot of water and toss in the balls. When they float to the surface, remove the balls and set aside to drain. Bring half the coconut cream to a boil, stirring constantly to prevent separation, then add flour balls. When mixture boils, remove from the heat and stir in remaining coconut cream. Serve in small bowls.

Assorted Desserts

157

158 *Sweet Rice with Fresh Mango*

Sweet Rice with Fresh Mango

1   cup sweet rice, soaked and steamed
1   cup coconut milk
½   cup sugar
¼   cup coconut cream
1   ripe mango
a pinch of salt

In a saucepan, combine all ingredients except for the steamed rice and the mango. Stir constantly for 3 minutes, or until sugar is dissolved, then add steamed rice. Cook for 10-15 minutes. Spoon the rice mixture into individual dishes and mold it into any desired shape. Peel mango and cut lengthwise, then use to surround the rice.

Sweet Rice Pudding

1   cup sweet rice, soaked and steamed
6   cups coconut milk
1   cup sugar
2   cups any fresh fruit or canned fruit cocktail
a pinch of salt

Bring coconut milk, sugar and salt to a boil, then add the rice. Stir for another 3 minutes, then add longans and spoon mixture into individual serving bowls.

Sweet Taro Pudding

2   cups taro root, peeled and cut into half-inch rounds
2   cups coconut milk
1   cup water
$\frac{1}{2}$ cup sugar
$\frac{1}{2}$ cup salt

Sauce:
1   cup coconut milk
$\frac{1}{2}$ teaspoon salt
$\frac{1}{4}$ teaspoon cornstarch
1   tablespoon water

In a saucepan, bring coconut milk and water to a boil. Add taro strips and cook for about 25 minutes, or until taro is soft, stirring occasionally. Stir in sugar and salt, and cook for another 10 minutes. Remove from heat and set aside.

For the sauce, heat the coconut milk, stirring until it boils. Stir in salt and cornstarch dissolved in water. Reduce heat to medium without allowing the mixture to boil. When sauce has thickened, remove from the fire and let cool in a serving bowl. Spoon sauce onto the taro pudding for individual servings.

Tapioca Delight

2	cups small tapioca pearls, soaked in water
10	cups water
3	cups sugar
4	cups coconut milk
1	cup canned jackfruit
1	cup canned longan
1	cup canned lychee
1	cup canned palm seed

a pinch of salt

Bring water to a boil. Add tapioca, stirring constantly. Let simmer until tapioca has softened. Combine all ingredients and cook another 5 minutes. Serve on individual plates.

Thai Custard

7	eggs
1	cup coconut milk
1	cup granulated sugar
1	teaspoon jasmine extract

In an oven, preheat a large cake pan with 2 inches of water at 375° F. Beat together eggs, coconut milk, sugar and jasmine. Pour mixture into a smaller cake pan and place in the preheated pan. Steam for half an hour or until done. Allow to cool and cut into slices before serving.

Water Chestnut Cooler

1   cup whole water chestnuts
1   cup tapioca flour
1   cup sugar
1   cup water with 2 drops of red food coloring
1   cup crushed ice
1   cup coconut cream
a pinch of salt

Quarter chestnuts and place in colored water, soaking them for 20 minutes. Drain and set aside. Roll chestnuts in tapioca flour and boil for a few minutes before placing in cold water. Mix sugar and water and bring to a boil, then set aside to cool. Combine drained water chestnuts with the sugar-water and crushed ice. Top with coconut cream mixed with salt.

Thai Desserts **163**

164 *Steamed Seafood with Wine*

MENUS FOR GROUPS

DINNER FOR FOUR

Thai Egg Rolls

Spicy Shrimp Soup

Eggplant Salad

Chicken Panang Curry

Mixed Vegetables with Beef

Steamed Rice

Sweet Rice Pudding with Longan Fruit

Tray of Fresh Fruits

DINNER FOR EIGHT

Butterflies

Hot and Sour Chicken with Coconut Milk

Thai Beef Salad

Ostrich Jungle King

Sizzling Salmon

Steamed Rice

Black Rice Pudding

Tray of Fresh Fruits

VEGETARIAN DINNER

Vegetarian Thai Egg Rolls

Spicy Vegetable Soup

Tofu with Greens and Shiitake Mushrooms

Hot Veggie Lover

Steamed Rice

Bananas with Coconut Milk

THAI STYLE COCKTAIL PARTY

Papaya or Mango Mimosa

Thai Egg Rolls

Thai Butterflies

Golden Prawns

Thai Crab Cakes

Satay Chicken with Peanut Sauce

Cucumber Salad

Mixed Fresh Tropical Fruits

Rice Cakes

SPECIALTY HOT DISHES

Seafood Spicy and Sour Soup

Spicy Grilled Beef Salad

Chicken with Chili and Basil

Spicy Noodles with Peppers

Green Curry with Pork and Eggplant

Chili Dipping Sauce with Fish Sauce and Cilantro

Steamed Rice

Commonly Used Vegetables

GLOSSARY

Agar

A gelatin from seaweed that gels desserts and cakes without refrigeration. Available in Asian grocery stores. Comes in little packets.

Bamboo Shoots

A crisp, cream-colored, conical-shaped vegetable used frequently in all Asian cooking. It is much simpler to buy the canned variety, which is readily available in all Asian stores and many Western supermarkets.

Basil

A strong and pungent herb. There are various types, but two varieties are used most often in Thai cooking: sweet basil (Horapa) and holy basil (Bai Kra Pow). Available fresh or dried in Asian and Western markets.

Bean Curd

Also known as Tofu, made from soybeans and available in Asian and Western markets either fried or fresh. The latter can be soft, medium or firm.

Bean Sauce

There are many kinds of bean sauces. The most common ones are yellow, black, and red bean sauces. Thai bean sauce is usually saltier than the Chinese or Japanese versions. In addition to beans, salt and sugar are also added.

Bean Sprouts

The sprouts of the green mung bean. Fresh sprouts are found in Asian and Western markets.

Black Mushrooms

Also known as Chinese mushrooms. When sold dried, however, they must be soaked in warm water for some time before using. The hard stems are discarded. Available in Asian and Western markets.

Black Rice A dark purple, long-grained, glutinous rice. Used mainly for desserts.

Cardamom Grown mainly in India and Ceylon, the dried seed pods are either pale green or brown, according to variety. Sometimes they are bleached white. They are added, either whole or crushed, to rice dishes and curries. Also used in desserts.

Cellophane Noodles Also known as "bean thread vermicelli," they are firm, transparent noodles made from mung beans. They are usually soaked in warm water for 5 minutes before use. They are also deep-fried straight from the packet, when used as a garnish.

Chilies Among the different spicy chilies are red and green serrano, red and green cayenne, and the jalapeños from Mexico.

Chinese Five-Spice Powder A combination of ground fennel, star anise, ginger, licorice root, cinnamon, and cloves.

Cilantro One of the most essential ingredients in Thai cuisine. The seeds, roots, and leaves are all used, and each has its own distinctive flavor. Also known as **Coriander**

Cinnamon Use cinnamon sticks rather than the ground spice, which loses its flavor when stored too long. It is used in both sweet and savory dishes.

Cloves Cloves are the dried flower buds of a tropical evergreen tree native to Southeast Asia.

Coconut Milk Freshly grated coconut is used to make coconut milk by adding water, squeezing and straining. Where fresh coconuts are not available, the unsweetened canned coconut milk from Thailand is also excellent, convenient, and available in Asian stores.

Coriander

One of the most essential ingredients in Thai cooking. The seeds, roots and leaves are all used and each has its own distinctive flavor. Also known as **Cilantro**

Corn, miniature

Also known as baby corn, it is available canned. An attractive addition to many dishes that need little or no cooking.

Cumin

It is the most essential ingredients in the preparation of curry. It is available in seed form or ground.

Dill

A member of the parsley family, it has small feathery leaves and yellow flowers. Dill leaves can be chopped finely, used fresh or dried, or sprinkled on soups, salads, and seafood. It has a clean odor faintly reminiscent of caraway.

Dried Shrimp Paste or Sauce

A pungent paste made from prawns, and used in many Southeast Asian recipes. It is sold in cans, jars, or flat slabs and will keep indefinitely. Known as *kapi* in Thailand.

Eggplant, Purple

Long and purple, sometimes known as Japanese eggplant. Four to five inches long, about two inches in diameter, this eggplant is very tasty and tender. Available in most supermarkets

Eggplant, Thai

Green and round in color, it is sometimes served raw with a shrimp paste dip or cooked in a curry. They range from the size and shape of a pea to a cucumber or a grapefruit.

Fish Sauce

Called *nam pla* in Thailand, a thin, salty, brownsauce used in Southeast Asian cooking to bring out the flavor in food.

Galanga

It is delicate in flavor with brown skin and creamy white flesh. It is sold in powder form or as a dried root in Asian markets. Also called *kha* in Thailand.

Ginger

It looks like a brown-skinned gnarled root, commonly pickled, crystallized, or made into a drink.

Glutinous Rice

A long-grained variety of rice known as sticky rice frequently used for rice desserts.

Jackfruit

This very sweet tropical fruit grown mainly in Southeast Asia and South America grows on tree trunks and can reach the size of watermelon.

Kaffir Lime or Fragrant Lime

Called *makrod* in Thai. The peel, juice, and leaves are used in Malaysian, Indonesian, and Thai cooking.

Krachai

Also known as lesser ginger. Has a subtle, lemony flavor that makes it quite different from common ginger.

Lemon Grass

An aromatic type of grass with a strong lemony fragrance, known as *serah*, it grows with a small bulbous root. Grated lemon peel can be used as a poor substitute. An absolutely essential ingredient of Thai cooking.

Mangoes

Available in many varieties, sizes, colors and tastes-from fresh green or fresh ripe to pickled, dried, and canned. As a snack, green mangoes are eaten with a fish sauce dip mixed with roasted ground rice, sugar, chilies, and sometimes shrimp paste.

Mint

The common round-leafed mint is the one most often used in Thai cooking.

Mushrooms, button Very common, found in any supermarkert, along with the crimini mushrooms

Mushrooms, dried

The flavor of these dried mushrooms is distinctive. Sizes range from 1 - 2 inches in diameter. They keep indefinitely when stored in tightly covered containers. Before using they must be soaked in warm water for 15 to 30 minutes. The best should be reserved for dishes in which the mushrooms are cooked whole.

Mushroom, straw

These are thin, leaf-like mushrooms available fresh or canned. They have a wonderful texture and should be used as soon as possible after the can in opened. An attractive addition to many dishes, they need little or no cooking.

Noodles, rice

Available in a variety of sizes. Those made from sticky rice sometimes referred to as rice sticks. Very fine strands made from long grain rice are often called vermicelli noodles. Before using in a dish, rice noodles are usually presoaked in warm water. For a crisp garnish or appetizer, fry rice noodles, a small amount at a time in hot oil. They puff up and whiten instantly.

Noodles, yellow

Usually made with flour and egg.

Nutmeg

Used in curries, sweets, and cakes. For a strong flavor, grate finely before using.

Ong Choi

The Thai name for this vegetable is *pak-boong*. Also known as Thai watercress. This green, smooth-leafed vegetable has a flavor milder than spinach and a texture similar to watercress.

173

Oyster sauce   Made from oysters cooked in salted water and soy sauce. Keeps well and adds a delicate flavor to meat and vegetable dishes.

Palm Sugar   A strong-flavored, dark sugar made from the sap of coconut palms and Palmyrah palms. Dark brown sugar can be substituted.

Pandan leaves   These long, flat, green leaves are either crushed or boiled to yield their flavor and color. Always remove prior to serving, except when cooking Fried Chicken in Pandanus Leaves. Used as flavoring in rice, chicken, curries, and sweets.

Papaya, Thai   Papayas come in many varieties in Thailand and range in size and shape. Thai green papaya salad comes mixed with long string beans and anchovy, dried shrimp powder, sugar, ground peanuts, raw pickled crabs and anchovy. Some use plain papaya with tomatoes, garlic, lime juice, and fish sauce. The ripe papaya is commonly served chilled as a dessert.

Plantain Banana   A long, fat banana that remains green-yellow even when ripe. It is the best of all cooking bananas, especially for desserts. Originally from South America, it is available in most supermarkets.

Radish, pickled and salted   Fresh white radish is sun-dried, then salted and stored for about one month before use. No refrigeration is required for the dark brown pickled radish. Use sparingly because it is very salty.

Rice, brown   This is rice that has been hulled but which has not lost its bran. Brown rice contains more nutrients than polished white rice.

Rice Flour

Ground rice that can be bought at Asian stores and health food stores. It gives a crispier texture when used in batters or other mixtures.

Rice, jasmine

The most commonly used steamed rice for meals.

Rice Papers

These round, paper-thin wrappers are made primarily from sticky rice. After being formed, the rice papers are dried. Dampen with water before use to make them pliable and ready for filling.

Rice vermicelli

These noodles are very thin, white threads made from rice flour.

Shallots

Small, brown-skinned or purplish members of the onion family, they have very strong flavors. Available in Asian stores or most supermarkets.

Shrimp Paste

Thick paste with grayish color and a very strong odor. If kept stored in a tightly closed jar in the refrigerator, it keeps indefinitely.

Soy Bean Paste

A condiment of salty taste made from soy beans.

Soy Sauce

Light soy sauces are lighter in color, thinner in consistency, and saltier than dark soy sauces. Dark soy sauce, or black soy sauce as they are often labeled, is sweetened with molasses. Use light soy for shrimp, chicken and pork; darker soy with red meat, for roasting, or for richer color in sauces. If too salty, dilute with water.

Sriracha Sauce

This Thai-style pepper sauce is made from chili peppers, salt, sugar and vinegar. Available not only hot and sour, but also sweet, it comes in bottles and is found in most Asian markets.

Tamarind The sour fruit is often used for cooking, but a sweeter version exists. It is shaped like a large broad bean with a brittle brown shell, inside of which are shiny dark seeds covered with brown flesh and is sold dried in packets. Tamarind liquid is used to add a distinctively sour taste and should only be used in small quantities.

Tapioca Flour Ground cassava root used for desserts and as a thickening agent in cooking. Readily available in most Asian markets.

Tofu Also known as **Bean Curd**, made from soybeans and available in Asian and Western markets.

Turmeric Powder Belonging to the ginger family, turmeric has an orange-yellow color and is used for sautés and curries, as well as in many other dishes.

Water Chestnuts Usually canned, but occasionally found fresh, water chestnuts have a crunchy texture. When fresh, their brown skin must be peeled off with a sharp knife and discarded.

THAI INGREDIENT SOURCES

ARIZONA
AJ's Finest Foods
7141 East Lincoln Drive
Scottsdale, AZ 85253
Tel. (602) 998-0052

CALIFORNIA
Bangkok Market, Inc.
4757 Melrose Ave.
Los Angeles, CA 90029
Tel. (213) 662-9705

Bezijan's Grocery, Inc.
4725 Santa Monica Blvd.
Los Angeles, CA 90012
Tel. (213) 662-1503

Jensen's Market
102 South Sunrise Way
Palm Springs, CA 92262
Tel. (619) 325-8282

Mo Hotta – Mo Betta
PO Box 4136
San Luis Obispo, CA 93403
Tel. (800) 544-4051

Taylor & Ng
1212B 19th St.
Oakland, CA 94607
Tel. (800) 255-3129

Thai Kitchen
PO Box 13242 Berkeley, CA 94701
Tel. (510) 268-0209

Yeen Sing Chong Company
977 North Broadway
Los Angeles, CA 90012
Tel. (213) 626-9619

CONNECTICUT
Bangkok Store
1932 Park St.
Hartford, CT 06106
Tel. (203) 236-7046

GEORGIA
Dekalb Farmers Market
3000 E. Ponce de Leon Ave.
Decatur, GA 30030
Tel. (404) 377-6400

ILLINOIS
Thailand Food Corp.
Thailand Plaza
481 N. Broadway St.
Chicago, IL 60460
Tel. (312) 728-1199

Thai Grocery Inc.
5014 N. Broadway
Chicago, IL 60640
Tel. (312) 769-0800

Thai Oriental Grocery
5124 S. Kedzie
Chicago, IL 60632
Tel. (312) 436-7381

LOUISIANA
Ho's Market and Parcel Service
1403 West Church Street
Hammond, LA 70401
(504) 542-1666

MARYLAND
Asian Food Inc.
2301 University Blvd. West
Wheaton, MD 20902
Tel. (301) 933-6071

Asian Food Market
615 S. Frederick Rd
Gaithersburg, MD 20877
Tel. (301) 948-1344

Nancy's Specialty Market
PO Box 327
Wye Mills, MD 21679
Tel. (800) 462-6291

Thai Market
902 Thayer Ave.
Silver Springs, MD 20912
Tel. (301) 495-2779

MASSACHUSETTS
Le Saucier Inc.
35 Eldridge Rd., Suite 209
Boston, MA 02130Tel. (617) 323-5015

Le Saucier
Faneuil Hall, Marketplace
Boston, MA 02109
Tel. (617) 227-9649

The Oriental Pantry
423 Great Rd.
Acton, MA 01720
Tel. (800) 828-0368

NEW JERSEY
The CMC Company
PO Drawer 322
Avalon, NJ 08202
Tel. (800) 262-2780

NEW MEXICO
The Chili Shop
109 East Water St.
Santa Fe, NM 87501
Tel. (505) 983-6080

NEW YORK
Aphrodisia Products, Inc.
282 Bleker St.
New York, NY 10014
Tel. (212) 989-6440

Bangkok Village Grocery Inc.
206 Thompson
New York, NY 10013
Tel. (212) 777 9272

Chinese American Trading Company
921 Mulberry St.
New York, NY 10013

Dean & Deluca
560 Broadway
New York, NY 10012
Tel. (212) 226-6800

Hot Stuff Spicy Food Service
227 Sullivan St.
New York, NY 10012
Tel. (212) 254-6120

House of Spices
76-17 Broadway,
Jackson Heights Queens, NY 11373
Tel. (212) 476-1577

Poo Ping Corp.
81 A Bayard St.
New York, NY 10013
Tel. (212) 349-7662

Siam Grocery
790 9th Ave.
New York, NY 10019
Tel. (212) 245-4660

OREGON
Anzen Japanese Foods and Imports
736 Northeast Union Ave.
Portland, OR 97232
Tel. (503) 233-5111

PENNSYLVANIA
De Wildt Imports Inc. RD #3
Bangor, PA 18013
Tel. (800) 338-3433

TEXAS
Asian Grocery
9191 Forest Ln. #3
Dallas, TX 75243
Tel. (214) 235-3038

Diho Market Texas Inc.
9280 Bellaire Blvd.
Houston, TX 77063
Tel. (713) 988-1881

Pendery's
1221 Manufacturing
Dallas, TX 75207
Tel. (800) 533-1870

Siam and Loaf Market
6929 Longpoint
Houston, TX 77055
Tel. (713) 681-0751

WASHINGTON
Asian Connection Store
409 Maynard S.
Seattle, WA 98144
Tel. (206) 587-6010

Asian Food Market
1832 W. Court St.
Pasco, WA 99301
Tel. (509) 547-8010

Beacon Market
2500 Beacon Ave. S.
Seattle, WA 98108
Tel. (206) 323-2050

Columbia Market
917 West Court St.
Pasco, WA 99301
Tel. (509) 545-1530

House of Rice
4112 University Way NE.
Seattle, WA 98105
Tel. (206) 545-6956

TNT Asian Market
208 E. Columbia Drive
Kennewick, WA 99336
Tel. (509) 586-9032

Uwajimaya Inc.
6th S. & S. King
Seattle, WA 98104
Tel. (206) 624-6248

Viet Hoa Market
676 S. Jackson
Seattle, WA 98144
Tel. (206) 621-8499

Welcome Supermarket
1200 S. Jackson
Seattle, WA 98144
Tel. (206) 329-7044

WYOMING
Spice Merchant
PO Box 524
Jackson Hole, WY 83001
Tel. (307) 733-7811

Index:

Qty.	Title	U.S. Price	Can. Price	Total
	Thai Cuisine At Its Best With Wine Recommendations	$16.95	$22.95	
	Subtotal			
	Shipping and Handling (add $4.00 for one book, $3.00 for each additional book)			
	Sales Tax (Wa residents only, add 8.6%)			
	Total enclosed			

Telephone Orders:
Call 1-8000-461-1931
Have your VISA or
MasterCard ready.

Fax Orders:
1-425-672-8597
Fill out order blank and fax.

Postal Orders:
Hara Publishing
P.O. Box 198732
Seattle, Wa 98109

E-mail:
harapub@foxinternet.net

Payment: Please Check One

☐ Check

☐ VISA

☐ MasterCard

Expiration Date _____

Card # _____

Name on Card _____

King and I Authentic Thai Cuisine

6030 Clearwater Avenue Kennewick, Wa. 99336 - Tel. 509 736-5464 / Fax. 509 783-1815

Name _____

Address _____

City _____ **State** _____ **Zip** _____

Daytime Phone: _____

Quantity discounts are available.
For more information, call (425) 776-3390
Thank you for your order!

Thai Beef Salad **185**